AN IRANIAN ODYSSEY

Gohar Kordi

SERPENT'S
TAIL

Library of Congress Catalog Card Number: 90-64191

British Library Cataloguing in Publication Data
Kordi, Gohar
    An Iranian Odyssey
    1. Iran. Social life, 1925–1979 -- Biographies
    I. Title
    955.052092

    ISBN 1-85242-213-0

First published 1991 by
Serpent's Tail, 4 Blackstock Mews, London N4
Cover design and illustration
by Bekah O'Neill
Set in 10/12½ Garamond by AKM Associates (UK) Ltd, Southall, London
Printed in Finland by
Werner Söderström Oy

I dedicate this book to my uncle Ezatollah Rahimifar.

Writing this book would not have been possible without the help and support of my husband David.

Gohar Kordi takes the name of Monir in this book; she has also changed the names of many of the characters.

125 rial is equivalent to £1 in today's currency.

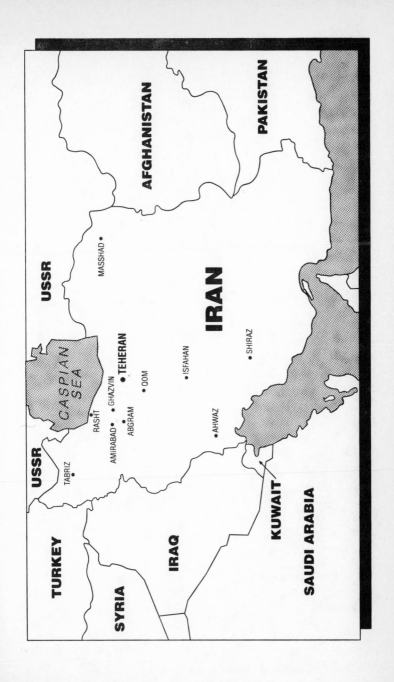

CHAPTER ONE

I must have been about four years old and I was playing outside in the street, when an older boy who would have been about seven, said to me, 'You can't see. You're blind.'

'No, I'm not,' I said confident, resolute.

'Yes, you are.'

'No, I'm not,' I repeated.

'If you're not,' he said, 'then drop that coin you have in your hand and pick it up.'

I dropped the coin and picked it up again straightaway. The boy walked off without a word.

I stood there with the coin in my hand, proud, triumphant. I had proved . . .

I wonder how long I went on with this illusion?

Maybe I still do not know that I am blind.

What happened during that period of my life?

It was as though the world came to a standstill. I was shut out. Doomed. Forgotten. I vegetated and yet lived. I was shut out from light, love, and wrapped in a curtain of darkness which lay all around me, touching me, squeezing me, hurting me, suffocating me.

Fear fills my heart, cripples me. I lose any attempt, any effort to struggle, protest.

I feel the bandages on my eyes, on my body, on my soul.

I dare not struggle, scream, protest — too dangerous. I have lost my voice. If I make the slightest protest the bandages will be pulled tighter and that will be the end of me.

Not a sound. 'She slept the whole time,' mother said.

If I were to meet my mother now, what would I say to her? I have a lot to say to you, mother, a lot! I want to show you some of my achievements. This is my son, meet him. Isn't he beautiful? And this is my husband. Isn't he handsome? And he loves me. I love him. Unlike you and your husband, you hated each other, didn't you?

And this is my house. Isn't it beautiful? Look, we've done it all by ourselves, my husband and I. It was a derelict house when we moved in. And look what we've made of it.

My son's room: — look we've just finished it. Decorated it, no, renovated it. I sanded it and scraped it with my own hands. Isn't it beautifully painted? The colour scheme, everyone says how beautiful it is. I can't see it.

But I want you to see it, mother. You tell me how nice it is.

People say this room is a child's paradise. Look at all these hand-made wooden toys. Aren't they beautiful to touch? I can't see them.

And his globe. He finds Iran, where I was born, on it. I can't see it.

Look at the carpets. Aren't they beautiful? Everyone admires them. Oriental, they think. They didn't cost much money and we did extremely well in finding them.

Everything is just so beautiful. Everyone says so. And I feel it, although I can't appreciate it to the full. I can't see it.

Look mother. I want you to see everything. See how well
I have done? I have given birth to this beautiful child, and
he is so wonderful. Such a perfect little boy. Sometimes
people are taken by surprise. 'Is he your child?' people
ask in dismay, just as people used to comment about me
when I was a little girl. 'Is this your daughter? But she is
beautiful!' You dressed me like a dolly, you said. Now I
understand how proud you must have felt. This was, of
course, before I lost my sight. With it I lost my beauty in
your eyes. In spite of that, I have done well, mother. I am
a good mother, mother. A good mother, unlike you. And
I am a good wife and a good friend, too. Friends say so.
After all, I haven't let you down, mother.

I said I lost my sight. No, I did not lose it. It was lost
for me. Did you do it, mother? You neglected me, didn't
you, because I was a girl. You neglected my sister as well,
and she died. I survived. Miracles happen, mother. How
come nothing happened to your sons? They were taken
good care of, because they were male. Isn't that right,
mother? Admit it. And, in doing so, free yourself from the
terrible guilt and free me from my anger.

I feel angry with you, mother. A terrible anger has been
locked inside me all these years and it has been eating
me away. It is time now to be released. I know, I know
you had a hard time. But I wasn't responsible for it. You
negated my existence because I was female. You put a
death-wish on me when I became blind, you said so
many times. 'I wish she was dead and had not recovered
from her illness!' And now look what I have done with
my life. Who were you to prejudge my future? 'What has
life got in store for her?' you used to say. I have not failed
you, mother.

Have a good look round my house. Oh, no, not in the

drawers, not yet, they are untidy, I have to sort them out. I want to show you good things about me for once. Look at my kitchen. I am a good cook, everyone says so, even my mother-in-law. They had a meal with us this Christmas for the first time. My mother-in-law, father-in-law, sister-in-law, brother-in-law, the lot, and I cooked them a good meal, they were most impressed. They enjoyed the visit. They didn't criticize anything as we feared they would. I proved myself. But look, I want to know what *you* think, mother, what would *you* say, have I done well?

Look at my curtains. Would you like to know how I got them? We didn't have money to get new ones. I rang the local library and asked them to read out jumble sales advertised in the local newspaper. Then I rang them to see if they had curtains and went round. Eventually I found a huge piece of curtain material. I found someone to make it to measure. They are all right, aren't they? People thought we had spent hundreds of pounds on them.

You see how I manage, do things, achieve? I can't see, but I have a mind and I use it, that is how I have survived despite what you put me through, mother.

I haven't told this to anyone before and I am telling you now: you've hurt me deeply, you've scarred me for life, you've crushed me but, look, I have survived.

I have no recollection of events early in my life such as my illness and before that of my sight. No visual memory except faint memories of colour, blues in particular, sky, maybe. I have blocked everything off, hidden the memories deep down, lost them, cannot find them even though I search.

What went through my mind during those three months of illness and then recovery? How did I feel?

When did I discover that I could see no longer? At what moment was that? How did I feel?

CHAPTER TWO

I was born on New Year's Day in Iran, *Norooz*, the twenty-first of March, the first day of spring. In Iran *Norooz* is a major celebration. People prepare months in advance. They spring-clean, buy new clothes, decorate and prepare delicacies. Having survived the harsh winter they celebrate, everything is cleaned and freshened, people wear their new clothes, especially the children. Children must have new clothes. If adults can't afford them somehow they manage for the children. They have to. Everyone tries to wear something new. People start visiting to wish each other Happy New Year, the senior members of the family first, grandparents, great uncles and aunts, senior members, who give presents to the young ones. Children receive coins from aunts and uncles, and coloured eggs and sweets from friends. Young married women receive a trayful of goodies from their parents and brothers — sweets, cakes, coloured eggs, a scarf, bits of jewellery maybe, and a piece of material for a dress, usually, or a chador, and this is called *pi*, a share, signifying that the women still play a part in their lives, that they have not been forgotten. Women who live far away receive their presents a few days before.

I was born early in the morning at about five o'clock. The news of my birth was taken to my father who stayed in a nearby house as was the custom in the village. Congratulations, it's a girl, the messenger shouted.

'Congratulations for a girl?' my father asked. The woman expected this response. She wasn't dismayed. The news had to be taken. She'd done her duty. 'It would have been better if a child had brought the news,' she thought, but it was too late. Had it been a boy it would have been totally different. The women would have argued over who was to take the news and she would have arrived breathless with running. 'You have a boy.' 'Wonderful,' he would laugh. 'Here.' And he would place a coin in her hand. He would go out and treat everyone in the neighbourhood to fruit or sweets. Everyone in the village would know that he had a boy. He would hold his head high, proud. In some cases, fathers of daughters would not return home for a while, or not speak to their wives for a time. What does a wife expect, giving birth to a girl? It wasn't too bad in my case, since luckily my father already had a son.

He was called Ali. I was called Monir. And then my second brother, Akbar, was born. Their last child was my sister, Khanomtaj.

Ali, the eldest, the first male, was always given special treatment. He was given the best of the soup, the best of everything. He was the family's hope, because he was male, the first son, the eldest. The first son was always regarded as the family's future security. He would carry the family burden, look after his parents in their old age. He was the life line of the generations. Daughters left home when married but sons stayed, even after they had married. The eldest son always stayed with the parents, and eventually took over the running of the household. There was great prestige in giving birth to a male child first. It was even more wonderful if the second and third were also male, just in case something happened to the first son. The parents would register the birth of a son late, thus their age was given as a few years younger on the birth certificate and the parents could benefit from having their son stay with them longer before he had to leave to do national service. On the other hand daughters were registered as a few years older than they actually were so they could be married off early. The legal age for marriage was fifteen so, a girl would often, in fact, be married at twelve. National service age for boys was at eighteen but they often went at twenty-one or twenty-two.

I do not know much about the first couple of years of my life except that my mother used to say, 'She was a beautiful girl before she lost her sight. She was so pretty, clever, full of life. I used to dress her like a doll. She could attract attention straightaway. "Whose daughter is this?" strangers would ask. "She's mine," I would say proudly. "Yours? What a beautiful daughter you have."'

'You know,' my mother would go on, 'that admiration did for her in the end. Yes, one of those people gave her the evil eye. That's why she lost her sight. Look at her, what is she now?

The words 'look at her' — and she said them often enough — made me feel diminished, worthless. And yet I said to myself, there is nothing wrong with me. I am here after all.

'She is not the girl she was,' mother would go on, 'she's totally changed, she's not the daughter I had.' The only time I received recognition, admiration, acceptance was when I still had my sight. Maybe that gave me the strength to fight for my survival later on.

At around the age of three I fell ill with smallpox. 'A disaster struck,' as my mother would often say, 'she was ill for three months. She did not open her eyes.' They bandaged them. 'She didn't cry, she just slept.' I just slept for three months. I must have been petrified. It was too dangerous for me to be awake, to make demands or protest. I felt the danger right to the bone. I demanded just enough to keep me alive, no more, no less. Female, I wasn't wanted in the first place and now how dare I ask for attention?

'After three months when we opened her eyes,' my mother would go on, 'she'd lost her sight in both. I wish she'd died really. Now look at her.' Those three words 'look at her' would always come up when she talked about me. I used to wonder if the other person was watching me then. I used to feel like hiding, going to sleep maybe, just as I slept those three months. I can imagine her, hear her voice when she opened my eyes and saw how damaged I was. I can feel the horror on her face, and hear her voice saying,

'As if having a girl wasn't bad enough, but a blind girl.' She repeated it often. 'What a misfortune. What have I done to be punished like this? What a burden on the family for life. An extra mouth to feed.' I often heard that — an extra mouth to feed — because being blind meant I'd also lost the chance of being married off.

Mother had one other story about my birth which she often talked about. 'She's *babghadam,*' she said of me. She believed that my arrival brought bad luck to the family. 'Anything we touched turned to stone after her birth, everything went wrong for us.' I never knew for sure what did go wrong although I understood that I had evil power and ought to be avoided, put away, to sleep forever maybe. This feeling that I had evil power was to have an enormous effect on my life. When I was about four or five, mother was talking to a woman about me and said, as usual, that I had brought bad luck. The other woman said, 'Don't say that in front of her.' 'Oh, she doesn't understand,' mother replied.

CHAPTER THREE

My mother's name was Mahi. She was born in a small Kurdish village named Khorbendeh. There were five children in the family, three boys and two girls, and she was the fourth child. She had been happy as a little girl in the village among her own people, until she had been married off against her wishes at the age of twelve, as was customary, to another Kurd from the next village. The marriage had not worked — that is to say, she had not allowed it to be consummated. She was eventually divorced and after a while was married off to my father, a Turk from a distant Turkish village, Kahleh, also against her wishes. Father's name was Reza. He was a good and gentle man, but mother did not love him; in fact, she hated him because she had already fallen in love long before, with a young Kurd from her own village.

It was the month of July, the height of the summer heat. People slept on the roof in the night for the coolness. Sometimes they ate their supper on the roof as well. One night after supper during which Mahi and Reza, her husband, had not spoken one word, she started to lay out the bedding. Bedding was normally kept on the roof in summer, folded into a pile and covered with a large cloth. She put two small mattresses down next to each other, just long enough and wide enough for the three of them. The little boy would go in the middle, Mahi would sleep on one side and her husband on the other. Then she put down the pillows, one small cushion in the middle for the boy and two pillows long and round, like sausages, on each side which she had brought with her as part of her dowry. Her mother had made them as mothers did for their daughters long before their marriage and stuffed them with all sorts of things, bits of raw wool, bits of left-over fabrics, some hair including her own, and bits of feather. Sometimes Mahi would stick her finger into the pillow to see what interesting things she could find in there. The mattresses were filled with old clothes, rags, bits of cottonwool, and wool sewn together. Then she put down a couple of folded quilts in case it became cool later in the night. The quilts were made of cotton wool. They also came with her dowry and had been made by her mother. She'd brought all the bedding with her when she married. Then she put the little boy in the middle and covered him with her old chador to protect him from the mosquitoes. She did this with care. She raised the chador over his face so that he could breathe easily. She stopped for a moment and looked at her son. She was clever to produce this first child, a boy. She would share her old chador with her son but she would not share anything with her husband, she would rather he slept at the other end of the roof, or even downstairs. If only she could leave his bed downstairs, as far away as possible from her. That would be ideal. But such hopes were fantastic and never went beyond wishful thinking. She handled the child with great care. Each time she touched him *Besmella he rohmanehnahim* she said, 'in the name of God'. He was a gift from God and should be handled with great care and respect. Every child was God given but this one was special to her, a boy, her first child. The family's hopes focused on him. He had to be well looked after and well cared for. Her second pregnancy had failed and she'd miscarried the year before. She didn't mind. She already had a boy. Many second pregnancies ended badly. She was very young, there was still time. Her first was three now so it was time for another child. People kept asking whether she was pregnant. Her mother, her sister. 'It's God's will. The time will come.' She took a last look at the child as he slept, deeply, peacefully.

There was still a lot to do before going to bed. She collected everything she had to take downstairs, the pot, bowls, spoons, the *sofreh*, the cloth the bread was wrapped in; she put them all on a tray, lifted it on to her head and started to climb down the ladder. That's how she carried things around. On her head. Holding the tray with one hand and holding the ladder with the other. The steps squeaked as she climbed down. She had to wash the dishes, make the dough for the next morning's bread, attend to the milk, make the cheese, and then mend her husband's trousers. She hated doing that. It wasn't the sewing she hated. She enjoyed sewing but she hated doing anything for him. She'd been putting it off for days while he grumbled and told friends she wasn't doing anything for him, not even mending his trousers. 'I feel I haven't got a wife,' he'd joke. 'Look at my trousers, they're still not mended.' She worked away gently, quietly. At times she sang to herself as she worked in the cool, fresh air of the evening. She enjoyed the peace and quiet of the evening, being on her own and taking things gently, quietly. She loved doing things in the garden in the moonlight. It didn't seem very long to her before everything was done.

Before going up to bed she had to say her prayers. She prayed three times a day, once in the morning before sunrise, once in the afternoon, and once in the evening after sunset — if she was menstruating or if she'd had intercourse, she had to go through the cleansing ritual before prayer. This was in three stages and was called *ghusl haze*. First she would place her head under running water, then she would stretch her right arm under the running water, then her left arm. She would accompany these gestures with the words: 'In *ghusl haze* I cleanse myself so that I may get close to the Lord.' Otherwise, she would take a jug, an *aftabeh*, of water into the toilet and wash between her legs, then squat in the garden and splash water on her face and on her arms three times. Then with two fingers of her right hand she marked her head and her feet repeating verses from the Koran. After this she was cleansed and ready to say her prayers. If she passed wind during prayer she would have to repeat the cleansing process. After cleansing, she put on her chador and fetched the prayer mat. She chose a spot in the middle of the room and stood facing north towards Mecca. There was one large mat and one medium and one smaller. She unrolled all three. Inside them she kept a *mohr*, a little rectangular block of clay from Mecca onto which she placed her forehead, a Koran prayer book, a *tasbeh*, with lots of beads also from Mecca, as well as a few other special items. She'd brought the prayer mats as part of her dowry. They were beautifully embroidered. The fabrics were from Mecca. She set them all out and started to pray. She had to bend down seven times, each time resting her forehead on the *mohr*. Sometimes she should say extra prayers for the days she had missed (for having a period), but this evening she didn't feel like saying more than seven, the necessary number. She wanted to get out up on to the roof as soon as she could, and look at the stars and the moon and enjoy the cool fresh air of the evening. When she had finished praying, she folded all the mats and put them away.

Before leaving the room she stood for a moment and wondered whether to take the trousers up with her. No, she didn't feel like it, she didn't feel up to it, she'd do it tomorrow, in the morning, in the daylight. She just wanted to get up there and let her mind drift and enjoy the coolness of the evening and look at the stars. She loved looking at the stars and just dreaming, letting her mind wander far away. She looked forward to that each evening. She longed for it. As usual, she felt lighter after saying her prayers, revived, happy, content and at peace with herself. She felt she'd been listened to, accepted and gained strength. No, she would leave the trousers, she would do them tomorrow, in the daylight. She promised herself she'd do them. She didn't even feel so angry with her husband now, after having said her prayers. What's more she felt a little ashamed for not having mended his trousers. She was his wife after all. It was the least she could do for him. It was a wife's duty to serve her husband. She took a last look around. She'd better take some drinking water upstairs. She closed the window and then locked the door. She picked up a copper bowl from a large basket where she'd left the dishes to dry, filled it with fresh water and climbed the ladder.

The steps squeaked as she went up. She put the bowl of water down next to her husband, and the key next to that. He would be going down later to say his prayers. He would know where the key was kept. They needn't talk to each other at all. During the day the little boy would carry messages between them, at times with disastrous results. 'Go and tell your father we're going to dinner at auntie's tonight,' or 'Go and tell mother we are having two visitors for dinner tonight.'

'Mother, father said to tell you we have two visitors for dinner tonight.' 'Your father be damned', mother replied and the little boy ran down the street in excitement, and said in a loud and clear voice, 'Mother said father be damned,' in front of the visitors. This meant trouble for her afterwards.

She watched over the boy. He was fine, he slept peacefully. She felt proud of him. She went to bed, adjusted her pillow and lay down covering herself and the boy with the chador.

She lay there on her back, looking at the stars, counting them. How many could she see? She'd seen the moon earlier in the evening. Whenever she saw the moon for the first time she always tried to look straight after at water or in a mirror for luck; and to avoid looking at the face of a person who was not a friend, which might mean bad luck. She always made sure not to look at her husband's face. She hated him. She looked far off into the distance, at the stars. Could she see? She tried to penetrate to the most distant, tiniest stars, taking her mind further and further away from her body. It was like flying. She felt so weightless. The sky was beautiful, full of stars. Occasionally a light breeze stroked her cheeks and brought her the fresh, pure smells of the country, of flowers and herbs. It was magical. Everything felt so beautiful, so perfect, so unique, complete. She let her mind float. She felt herself lifted, going further away from the earth, excited, liberated, enriched. She felt part of it all, and yet in control. She went over and above everything, everything she'd known, everything she'd experienced. She felt the joy, the happiness, deep down inside her, which nourished her, cherished her, fulfilled her. This was ultimate beauty, perfection, and she saw herself as part of it all. She was young, beautiful, healthy, full of energy. She was creative, clever, capable. She saw herself as powerful. Nothing could limit her, restrict her, cut her down, not even her husband or the landlord, or her mother. No one could tell her what to do or how to be. She would decide what to do, how to be, what to be. She was in charge, in control of herself. Just like the nature she saw around her, part of nature and yet apart, powerful. She felt wonderful. Her dreams carried her away into the night. She was happy sleeping on the roof in the open. Here she was safe. All the neighbours slept on their roofs. He dare not touch her. She would protest. They would hear. He knew this, so never touched her. People slept all around her. She slept with them in mind. Their presence gave her a sense of security, safety, peace. With her family she slept together and yet apart — with the neighbours she slept apart and yet together. She was pleased to get to bed, she sighed with relief, the day was over and now she could be herself. She could dream, sleep, escape. In a moment all her tensions, all her exhaustion, her anxiety, would be over.

She flew and flew, seeing everything and everyone. All the villages she'd been to, all the weddings, the gatherings, the celebrations she had attended, she saw them all. But she was looking for someone. Someone she knew, someone she loved, who was expecting her, waiting for her, longing for her. She knew this well. She had to search. She had to find him, amongst all these people and all these things. He had to be somewhere. She would find him, she was sure of that. He was waiting for her and she would find him. She moved along looking, searching, with all her body, all her mind, all her soul. The whole of her needed the whole of him, her childhood sweetheart, Assim.

She had met Assim a long time ago, when she was a little girl taking part in a festival in the fields outside the village, the festival held on the thirteenth day of the New Year to let the evil out of life and welcome the good. She'd danced with him in her tribal Kurdish costume. They'd sung together, danced together, to the music, with the flowers around them. She'd thrown handfuls of fresh grass over her shoulder as was the custom and recited a poem expressing the desire that this time next year she would be married and live in her husband's house with a child in her arms. She had recited it like other young girls without knowing its true meaning. She did not know then who her husband would be.

The husband who had been arranged for her was a disaster. Now in her dream she was looking for the true one, the one she'd chosen a long time ago, Assim. Assim had lived in the same village. He was a Kurd, like herself but fate had separated them. She dreamt about him all the time. He'd been in her mind and in her heart since that first meeting when she was a little girl. They were meant for each other. They knew that. They had sworn to be together for ever. Because of her promise she'd not allowed her first marriage to be consummated and she'd been divorced and later remarried to another man, my father, a Turk from a distant village. Her first husband was not from her own tribe. He was a complete stranger. Assim was her own. She'd chosen him. He'd chosen her. They belonged to each other. They longed for each other. They'd danced together. They'd sung together. They'd laughed together. They'd played together. They'd held each other. They'd touched each other, through their language, dance and customs. They'd looked at each other and reached out to each other. They'd made a contract to wait for each other, only for each other. Ever since that first meeting, whenever she'd been to weddings, celebrations, visits, she had always looked for him, hoped to see him. She'd dressed for him, she'd danced for him, she'd laughed for him, she'd longed for him. They met many times. Those times had been the happiest of her life. She'd danced for him with all her strength, all her might, all her desire. He'd looked to her, right inside her. She remembered a wedding where she'd been dressed in her brilliantly coloured Kurdish costume waiting for him restlessly. Where is he? Why is he late? She could hear her heart beat and feel the flush on her cheeks and suddenly he'd arrived, wearing his own Kurdish costume. She remembered how she had wanted to throw herself into his arms and seen his desire to draw her to him, to squeeze her tight. Instead she'd felt the tears in her eyes and had complained of the heat. His late arrival suddenly seemed all right, she'd forgiven him, he could no nothing wrong. Anything he said was perfect. The perfection was in him, they were one, they were perfect. In her costume stitched with gold and silver coins, a waistcoat in satin, a pretty blouse, a short skirt heavily gathered at the waist, brightly coloured ribbons in her hair, she looked beautiful, desirable. Her happiness, joy, pleasure radiated.

She was flying around looking for him, her hair all in plaits, many plaits. She flew through all those villages and eventually found his village. There. He was there at the crossroads near the boundary of her parents' village. He was waiting, looking around him, a bit anxious, tired maybe. She shouted, 'Here I am, Assim, it is me, I've come for you, you're waiting for me, I know, here I am.' He looked up.

Now after all these years she saw him as on that wedding day, standing looking one way and then the other. He didn't seem impatient. Just tired. His costume was dusty, his face tired. He seemed to be waiting for someone special, precious, it was as if he would wait for ever. Suddenly he stopped searching, and concentrated. He listened. He'd sense her presence. 'Assim, I have come to you, I have found you, you've been waiting for me, I knew this, here we are together.' He looked up and saw her right above in the sky. 'But how do I get to you?' he said anxiously. His face lit up. Their eyes flashed. Her voice strengthened. 'I'll drop my plaits. You tie them round your waist and I'll pull you up,' she said confidently. Then she dropped her many plaits. He tied them round his waist and she pulled him up.

Her marriage to Reza had been arranged quickly. She'd been resigned, realizing that nothing would change her parents' mind. She'd brought shame on them already. She had to go through with it this time. When she slept with her husband for the first time, she did not resist, she did not fight. She imagined that she was with Assim in order to make light the pain and discomfort. A woman stood outside the room, waiting for the consummation of their marriage. She would take out the stained towel, the sign of her virginity, to the senior women of both families. Afterwards both families were relieved, especially her own. At last, their daughter had shown some sense, had conformed, had performed, had obeyed like a good woman.

From then on every time her husband made love to her she imagined it was Assim. Otherwise she could not have gone through with it. This was her method of survival. Afterwards she always dreamt of Assim and in her dream she gained satisfaction from him, from her true lover. This was how it carried on. She gained a sense of lovemaking, of satisfaction, of fulfilment, from her dream. Her dreams became the most important part of her life, life giving, sustaining, energizing. She lived with Assim in dreams. This was her real life, real love, real existence. She carried an image of him with her everywhere. She would have daydreams any time, anywhere, whether she was carrying water from the stream or doing her washing in the river. Milking the goats in the early morning, she would think of him, hear him, feel him. She fantasized that one day Assim would take her far away from her husband, from the landlord, from all her worries. Or that she would run away and look for him, and they would leave together, they would go somewhere beautiful, restful, peaceful. They would build a fine house for themselves, and have many children, they would be happy, the happiest family on the earth. She lived with this dream. This was her secret.

'You are not here, Mahi,' her friends would sometimes say laughing. She was called Mahi because she was beautiful, magical, like the fish in the rivers which were admired, but never caught. 'You are always dreaming, Mahi, what are you dreaming of? You never tell us, what you think.' 'Oh I was just thinking of my mother,' she would say with a big sigh. 'That's not it, surely you're hiding something from us.' 'You don't understand,' she would say sometimes, 'your mothers are not so far away from you. I have none of my family near me, it takes one whole day to get to her village on a donkey. You can see your mother many times a day. Me, only once or twice every few months. So, I dream about her.' It was a good opportunity for her to let off steam, to moan, to express her need, her desire, the loss of her mother and family on one level and of Assim on the other.

The birds starting to sing. She was gaining consciousness, waking up to the realities of the world. She listened for her boy's breathing as she always did. He was all right. The ladder squeaked. Her husband was going down to morning prayer. She dreaded her daily encounters with him. She hated him. She had to face another day with him. She tried to get back to her unconscious world, she closed her eyes and tried to shift to her dream world for a few more moments. She kept coming in and out of consciousness, waking up, going back. The man, her husband, was trying to wake her up. 'It's prayer time,' he whispered, lifting the cover off her face. She pushed him away and covered her face. She was angry. 'The sun will rise in a minute, you have to get up.' 'Leave me alone,' she said.

'Everybody's up,' he whispered. 'I suppose I have to get up. What will the neighbours think?' she said to herself. She waited another couple of minutes for him to move away. This he did. She had to get up. She looked at the boy, he was all right, she covered his face again, took up the bowl of water, and the light and climbed down the squeaky ladder. She was cross and anxious, cautious. She filled the jug with water, went to the toilet, washed herself, then out in the yard she washed her face and her arms three times, marked her head and feet, and then put on her chador, put down the prayer mat and faced north.

She wanted to get out of the room as soon as possible. Her husband entered and closed the door behind him and her heart sank. What did he have in mind? Should she run out? Or prolong her prayer? She folded up the prayer mat quickly, and put it on the fireplace, trying to avoid his gaze. She went towards the door but he grabbed her. 'Come here my darling.' He pulled her to himself. 'Leave me alone,' she shouted in anger, 'get out, let me go.' 'Sssshhh, the neighbours will hear you.' She started fighting. She kicked him and bit his hand. He held her firm and drew her closer to him, and kissed her whenever he could. He held her tight for a moment. 'I hate you.' 'I know. You haven't told me why. What have I done, heh?' She kept silent, didn't know what to say. She didn't have anything to say. He kissed her again and lay her down gently, firmly. 'Let me go, leave me alone, go away.' 'I will in a minute.' He held her tight. 'Sshh, the neighbours will hear you. What would they think?' 'Ha, ha, ha,' he laughed, 'I don't care.' 'I hate you.' 'I know, I love you, my beauty, you haven't told me why you hate me. Heh? Tell me what have I done?' 'I don't know, I just hate you, you hurt me.' He kissed her again. 'Come here my darling, I'm your husband, you are my wife, do you know what that means?' She kept quiet. She knew what this meant, as his wife he had the right to make love to her as often as he liked. She was obliged to provide this service. She had to serve her husband. 'The child, the child is on the roof.' 'The child is all right,' he whispered. Squeezing her tighter, running his hand up her legs, he took her trousers off. She struck out, she kicked. She was small but strong and determined. He was stronger. 'It's my period.' 'Your period was three weeks ago. One more week to go! Ha ha ha,' he laughed. 'You think I don't know the dates? You say that every time, don't you?' He laid her in the right position for him. She tried to scream. He held her mouth. 'Ssshh, darling, the neighbours.' She bit his hand and managed to free her mouth. 'Your father be damned,' she uttered as he entered her, and with those words he felt stabbed in the heart. He carried on. There, she'd done it. That was the worst thing she could have said to him, the worst thing any woman could say to a man. Out with it. Right into his heart where it hurts most. As though this made it easier for her, within a few moments the act was over. She felt dirty, violated, polluted. He felt insulted, deeply hurt.

How dare she say such a thing about my father. I'll show her what this means. She'll not get away with it. I'll teach her a lesson. You just wait, you bitch. Both of them were angry. Her first thought was to cleanse herself. She had to go to the baths today and completely cleanse herself. This was the last time ever he would touch her. She would not let this happen ever again.

The *hamam*, public baths, stood in the centre of the village. On certain days of the week it was open to men and on others to women. That day it was open to women. Later that morning, she prepared to go to the baths. In a large square embroidered cloth she bundled all the things she wanted to take with her. A change of clothes for herself and a change of clothes for the boy. She put henna on her hair every three months, and now it was time to do it again. Henna nourishes the hair, makes it healthy, silky. If it wasn't applied regularly women would complain of headaches. She would put it on in the bath and sit for a couple of hours waiting for it to take effect. She began to bundle her things together. She took some special clay for washing the hair (*gellsar*). Then she took a scrubber, a pumice stone to scrub her feet, and a clay ball to rub over her skin to remove the dead cells, and a comb, some cotton fabric as a flannel and a herbal hair removing cream. She put in a *longue*, a large rectangular cloth to cover herself from the waist downwards, a large towel to use as a bath mat, a bowl, some soap and the henna. She put in a loaf of bread as a payment for the bath.

She took her big bundle and went to see whether the neighbours were going to the baths. One neighbour would agree to pick up the children from the bath so the other could have a longer time for herself. What would she do for dinner? She couldn't be bothered to think about it. She would do something quick in the evening. Going to the bath was a big event lasting three to four hours. Women usually went with a friend or neighbour and, with just each other for company, they would have a good talk.

Women chatted together all the time. They poured out their troubles to each other, nothing was secret or private, everything was talked about and discussed — their miseries, their joys, the cruelties, the injustices. They shared them, listened, sympathized, comforted, soothed and cried with each other and for each other. Their lives were made public. They shared out their feelings, both negative and positive, their joys, their pleasures and their sorrows. Women could not share their unhappiness with their men but they could with each other. They could not take out their anger towards the men but they talked about it to each other. They could not control men or reason with them, or deal with them on an equal level, but their anger and frustration was vented in words, expressed, listened to, understood. This enabled them to carry on. They visited their relatives as often as possible and women living far away went and stayed with their parents for a week or two every few months, and during those visits they talked and talked. They had a good clean out. Then they felt recovered, revived, revitalized and able to carry on. Nothing was kept private or bottled up.

During a birth the house would be full of women of all ages, and children who would see everything, experience everything. All major events, birth, illness, death, the brutalities, the cruelty

AN IRANIAN ODYSSEY 27

that went on were all talked about many times. When my father died I was still a child and the women hit themselves on the head and cried aloud, alongside mother. The whole neighbourhood was there. Mother was not left alone. They would take turns to make sure someone was always there with her. Mourning was not a private, lonely matter. It was shared. It was public. It continued for seven days. It was the same for a birth. For seven days people would come and go, making sure there were always a couple of women around. The woman's mother would stay for a month. On the seventh day they would take the woman to the baths and after that it would ease off. There were always gatherings. Women did their work in groups and as they worked they talked. They did their washing together by the river, they fetched water together from the well in the evenings, they went to the bath together, they wove carpets together. Their sewing, knitting, mending, they did together in groups. It was a togetherness that gave them strength, especially in the bath as they talked and cleansed themselves.

After the bath that day Mahi went to her friends who had picked up the boy. They had tea while she recovered from her lengthy cleansing session. Towards evening she headed home feeling refreshed. She did not get round to preparing the dinner until quite late, busy with her other tasks, seeing to the goats, milking them, tending the chickens, bedding them and so on. Her husband arrived demanding dinner. When he heard it wasn't ready, he took his revenge. It was the excuse he'd been waiting for. He gave her a good beating, a severe one. You dare swear about my father, he said to himself as he beat her on her back and all over her body, specially her buttocks, where the bruises would be hidden. He hit her as hard as he could and left the house. Her screams had alerted the neighbours, who arrived and took her into their house with the boy. She was ill for some days and a message was sent to her mother to come and collect her. She spent a month at her mother's. She ached all over, especially her back. She was massaged frequently with special oils, given hot baths and herbal treatments. Once her husband arrived to fetch her but she wasn't well enough to travel and the family insisted that she should stay with them a little longer, until eventually it was time for her to come home. Her husband took her back as was the custom — the mother takes the woman away and then the husband comes to take her back. This was how it was done. On her return she discovered she was pregnant.

CHAPTER FOUR

We are in Khorbendeh, my mother's village, I am about four years old. I'm playing with an older boy of about seven out in the street and I have a coin in my hand. The boy says, 'You can't see.' 'Yes, I can,' I reply. 'No, you can't.' 'Yes, I can,' I insist. 'If you can, then drop that coin in your hand and pick it up,' he says. I drop the coin and pick it up straightaway. The boy walks away without a word, and I stand there, triumphant.

I did not accept the fact that I could not see. I performed the task set for me beautifully. On another level that was the moment when I understood that I could not see. I do not remember anything before or for long after that event. It stands out in my memory as clearly as though it were yesterday, the dusty street, the quietness, the boy's voice, his age. I have no recollection of my illness nor of my recovery, just as I have no clear recollection of myself as sighted, being dressed like a doll and admired. I believe the event happened after we moved to Khorbendeh to live with my mother's family. The reason for our move was that my father had been arrested and accused of spying by the Russian soldiers who occupied the country after the Second World War. Iran was occupied by both the Russians and by the British. I do not know whether my father was accused of spying for the British or the Iranian government, although I suspect it was for the British. He was kept in captivity for forty-five days and three times came close to being shot. Twice the soldiers changed their minds at the last minute. On the third occasion my father said his prayer and faced the wall as he was told, but the gun did not go off and his life was spared. He'd been tortured under interrogation. I used to feel the marks and scars of his torture, the dips and bumps on his head. He had severe headaches after that. I think my mother had given him up for dead and we moved in with her parents. He was ill for some time after his release. He didn't talk much about his experience in the hands of the Russians, but he expressed a deep contempt for them. He believed that God had saved his life, and that his release was the work of God. He was a melancholic man, frail, sensitive, weak. His torture and detention had long-lasting effects. He was often ill, depressed, especially towards the end of his life. They broke his spirit, demoralized him. He looked pathetic at times. My earliest memory of being with him, I must have been around two, is of sitting on his lap. He's feeding me grated carrot. He's saying to me, my angel, my beautiful girl, my sweetheart. I do not remember his face, but I do remember his voice, the warmth of his body and the taste of the carrot. The touch of the carrot, the shape of it, I remember, and the feeling of contentment. His touch, his voice, his smell, his words, his warmth, is right with me. I am one with him. He's happy, proud, lively. That's the happiest memory I have of him as well as the happiest memory of myself. Did he love me then because I was sighted, I wonder. Otherwise I do not remember father happy.

He used to travel a lot looking for work. He'd be away for months, and come back empty handed as mother put it. He's just hopeless mother would say, he can't make anything out of anything. He used to go to other villages selling goods, but he was too generous, he would give things away, so he would not make any profit. 'God is great,' he would say, 'what I give today I will receive tomorrow.' But, according to mother, nothing was ever received. She saw him as a good for nothing. Mother used to repeat what he said and laugh sarcastically. 'He thinks he's clever.

He says if he bangs two stones together he will get something out of it, or if he lifts one stone off another he'll find gold between them. Fool. If someone gives him notes galore, he'll give them to the wind. He's inadequate, incapable, hopeless. What bad luck I had. Marrying him was the worst thing that could have happened. It's my fate. I'm unlucky. He doesn't realize what I do. I've scraped together to make a home for him, he leaves me for months on end with nothing, I have a terrible time trying to keep the wolf from the door.' And she was right.

I don't know anything about father's parents, I never met them. He had a younger brother, Norooz Gholi, in a nearby village, who often visited us and always brought us sweets and presents. Uncle Gholi was a quiet, gentle person, affectionate and caring. Mother liked him. He also had two sisters, Zolikha the elder, and Asli the younger sister, who both lived in our village. Aunt Zolikha liked me particularly. Perhaps she was the only woman who gave me unconditional love in my early life. I was heartbroken when we moved from our village, to Teheran, leaving her behind. She was kind and caring. She felt sorry for me. I remember her voice, which was gentle, kind and soothing. She always paid special attention to me. I seemed to be her favourite, I felt comfortable with her and happy in her presence in a way I never felt with my mother. With mother I felt uncomfortable and awkward, as though I shouldn't have been there.

In the little village where I was born, Kahleh, father's village, the people all spoke Turkish. Mother's village was Kurdish speaking. Kahleh was a little primitive, hilly, barren wild village. We had to leave Kahleh and move to Teheran because of a cruel landlord. Stories of the cruelty of landlords were horrific. Brides were raped on their wedding nights by landlords, and it was said that young women raped by landlords were taken by the latters' wives, put in sacks and tortured with large needles until they lost consciousness. One story which made a special impression on me was of a man with failing sight who did not recognize the landlord approaching him and did not stand up. He was publicly whipped. That story petrified me.

The house in Kahleh I remember was one large room about fifteen by thirty feet, long and narrow, with thick walls. We used to sit on a very wide windowsill — it was about eighteen inches wide. There was also one little window, with a wooden window frame but no glass, and about seven or eight smaller windows, maybe ten inches across, like holes in the roof, which were covered at night by bricks. In the morning mother would take a long stick and push them open. At the window end of this room was the *tanoor*, the oven in the ground. The *tanoor* was made of clay and then put into a hole dug in the ground. This was the focal point of the house. It was used for heating the house, for cooking, for baking. In the winter it was kept alight for twenty-four hours. Mother used to clean it out every morning, then light a new fire and bake her bread, after which she put back the *korsi*. The *korsi* was a very large stool placed over the oven. Then she draped a large quilt over the *korsi*, and a large bedspread over that. Small mattresses were laid around the sides of the stove, for seats. Larger cushions were laid against the walls so we could sit round the *korsi* pulling the quilt over our legs to keep warm. Meals were served over the *korsi* which was first covered with a *sufreh* (tablecloth) in which the bread was wrapped. At night we slept on the mattresses round the *korsi* pulling the quilt over us. In summer the *korsi* was taken away, and the oven was covered by a piece of wood, shaped to size, then the bedding was made into large cushions and laid against the walls. I used to help mother make up these bundles every morning for people to lean on.

At the other end of the room stood containers made from clay, painted and used for storage. They were about eighteen inches across and of different lengths, a tall one for wheat, another tall one for barley, one for flour, another for bread, then a little one for salt. They stood on legs with a hole in the bottom and a stopper which came out. You would take out the quantity of grain you wanted, and then replace the stopper. The containers stood near the wall, with other goodies behind and there was just about space to move around between them. In the centre of the room was a large square space for activities such as making butter. For that we had a large pouch or churn made of animal skin, called a *tulwgh*, into which diluted yoghurt was poured. The two ends of the *tulwgh* were hung from the ceiling. Two people, one at either end, would swing the *tulwgh* backwards and forwards with great force. After half an hour, mother would open the *tulwgh* and take out the lumps of butter. To get the *tulwgh* going, she needed help. A neighbour came in to help her fill it, hang it and then swing it. After the butter was removed the remaining liquid was strained. Once strained, it was very thick. They formed this into balls, called *kashk* which were dried in the sun and kept. In winter, the *kashk* would be soaked and dissolved until it was custard-like and ready to be used in cooking. The butter was kept salted until there was enough for it to be heated and made into oil which smelled absolutely wonderful. If a little heated oil was put on the rice, anyone could smell it houses away.

In our case the oil was saved and given to the landlord like the cheese and the wool from the sheep, the eggs from the chickens, and all the other animal products. The animals belonged to the landlord. My mother just looked after them. She would look after seven or eight lambs and goats each summer and in return she would receive a tiny percentage of the produce, so little it was hardly noticeable. Landlords were known to be cruel. Cruelty was the norm. If a landlord showed any leniency, or kindness, it was talked about for months and months.

The frame for carpet making was on the side of the room by the window. In winter the landlord gave mother all the materials and mother would make the carpet. It took months. Through the long winter nights mother used to sit and weave away, stitch by stitch. Sometimes she sang to herself while weaving. At times her friends and neighbours would come in to give her a hand for an hour or two. She did the same for them. She made beautiful carpets. The landlords were very happy with them. Her designs were exquisite. She was artistic, imaginative, creative. On one occasion, after finishing a carpet she took it to the landlord and returned deeply disappointed. 'The *arbab* [landlord] couldn't stop admiring it,' she told us. 'He kept walking up and down on it, saying what beautiful work. This is the best I've seen for a long time. Wonderful. Who's done it?' This woman here, he was informed. He glanced at mother. 'All right, give her eight pounds of barley.' 'Barley!' she kept repeating. 'Couldn't he at least have given me wheat? He couldn't stop admiring it and yet he gives me barley, and only eight pounds. Cruel man. He has no heart, has he? My fingers still hurt and my eyes burn from all those sleepless nights I spent making it. Couldn't he have given me wheat? He couldn't stop admiring it, and yet he gives me barley.' She couldn't stop talking about it, and repeating the story over and over again. She was hurt. Her work had been appreciated but not rewarded. She felt the injustice right to her bones. Did that kind of treatment make her bitter? Did she take out the bitterness on father?

During the day a shepherd would take the animals out of the village to the fields and in the evening would return to the centre of the village with them. Then the sheep would find their own way to their houses. Sometimes a particular goat or lamb wouldn't turn up, or was late, so mother would go out to look for it, shouting through the open doors, 'Is that our black and white goat? Come here, ah that's it, come home.' And she would bring the animal home to its little house the size of a large room above the cellar, where the donkey was kept. There was a section for the kids or the lambs with a little wall around it. Once inside the stable, mother let the young suck for a minute or two before milking the goats or sheep. I helped mother take the young animals away to their walled shelter and they would scream as I pulled them away from the teats. Why not let them suck longer, I used to ask myself. I felt it was unjust but I had to do it. Once we got all the young out of the way then it was milking time. I held the head of the animals while mother milked them. She put a big copper bowl underneath and, having first washed her hands, chanted *Besmella he rohmanehnahim* 'in the name of God'. She always said that when she handled food, and babies or children, especially if they weren't well. She would start the milking. 'Oh wonderful' she would remark occasionally, 'tonight this one has given so much milk.' When the bowl was full she would empty it into a bucket and start again. We would go from one to the other until seven or eight sheep were all milked. 'Good, well done, that's lovely,' she would praise them. I would still feel sorry for the young for not having enough milk.

I didn't get enough to eat. The best of the soup went to the boys. First to my older brother, who was always given the most and the best of everything. He was a growing boy and he had to be fed well, as well as we could afford. And then to my father who, because he worked, needed a lot of food. And then to my younger brother, Akbar. And then anything left over was for me and my mother. I must have always looked hungry. Once when we had some visitors while my mother was preparing food, she scolded me for the way I sat with my head on my shoulder. I looked 'as though I'd never been fed,' she said, and that embarrassed her, so she gave me some of the food she had prepared, and said, 'never, ever do that again.' I could not enjoy the food. It was a revelation to me that my need had been expressed by the way I sat. I was surprised. How had they understood?

Mother had an arrangement with three or four other households. The women took the milk to each house in turn for a week, every morning and every evening. I could hear the women measuring out the milk. They made a mental note of how many bowls each person got in a day, and totalled the number as the days went on. By sharing, it was easier to increase the productivity.

Once I remember benefiting from that milk. I remember I was very little, maybe four years old, out playing with Akbar in the fields, when we ate some poisonous berries. We fell ill. The remedy mother used for us was lots of milk. For three days we were very ill and drank gallons of milk. I felt I was valued being given so much milk. I was cared for just as my younger brother was cared for, with the same amount of milk. That was one of the two occasions in my life I remember mother caring for and nourishing me. The other was when we had a severe thunderstorm. Akbar and I were out in the yard when it happened. There was thunder, lightning. It was very frightening. Mother came and sat on the floor in front of us and held both of us in her arms and started saying prayers. I felt equal then with my brother. She cared for me just as she cared for him. She prayed for me just as she did for him. I never forgot these two occasions when I felt of value.

Father used to leave us for months when looking for work in other villages, but mother somehow managed to feed us with her cheese and carpet making. There wasn't much to do in the village after the summer. Once the harvest was over father travelled to the other villages, to buy and sell, to barter — for example, a bag of wheat was exchanged for some tea or potatoes for a bar of soap.

My aunt Zolikha who was very fond of me always carried some sweets, raisins or nuts or dry dates, in her pocket and would take out a handful and give them to me, putting them in my lap. It was the custom that aunts or uncles or grandparents always had something in their pockets for the children. We looked forward to that. Asli, my younger aunt, was jolly, happy and outgoing, and always joking. I remember the voice. She was always laughing. She had two or three children. Both aunts lived maybe ten minutes' walk from our house. The walk was full of thorns and dips and hills, and sometimes I used to lose my way when I went there, or my bare feet would hurt from stones and the thorns. I used to fantasize that one day there would be a straight line, a raised, smooth pathway to their house that would take me right there so I wouldn't have to wander. This image was so fixed in my mind. When later in life I came across railway lines for the first time, they were like my image. The railway line would go straight there, just wide enough for me to walk on. I was sure in my mind that one day this path would be created. I used to dream a lot. I walked barefoot of course. We all did. Always. Summer and winter, so my feet used to be bruised and cut by sharp stones and thorns. I remember when I first walked on a railway line. It was so familiar, just as I had always imagined it as a little girl.

Akbar and I used to play in the river by our house. We used to try and build a kind of island in the river with the big river stones, and a bridge over to it. We used to walk in the river, play around, for hours. Once we took our tray — a large round heavy copper tray, maybe the most expensive item in the house, to the river and somehow the tide took it from us and it floated under the bridge and stuck where we couldn't get to it. We told mother and I remember she and a neighbour came and somehow got it out. We weren't told off, which surprised me. Mother never restricted my explorations because I couldn't see and I'm grateful to her for that. She never prevented me from going anywhere or stopped me playing with things or handling things, and that's been a great asset to me — just daring to go for things, to have a go, before deciding whether I can manage or not. I wonder whether it was because she wanted me to learn everything and have fun like my brother Akbar, or whether she didn't care what happened to me.

At the other end of the yard lived a brother and sister in their late twenties. Neither were married. They had their own entrance. The sister used to be there always but her brother used to go away. Once after he came back, she brought us some bread. That was the custom. If a husband came back from a trip it was expected that he would be the one to give something to a neighbour. Bread was the most usual thing to give. She brought us a few loaves saying: 'My brother's just come home this minute. I've brought you this. He doesn't know. I'm sure he will tell me to bring you some more later.' My mother was pleased and a day later we received some more which he'd asked her to bring us. Then they asked us for a meal one evening. We went to their house and had supper with them. The brother wasn't there, only the sister. There was mother and we children. We had *abgusht*, a kind of soup with lamb, chick peas, kidney beans, potatoes, tomato puree and onion, cooked slowly in the oven for five or six hours. First we were served the gravy in a bowl, and given lots of bits of bread to dip in and soak up the gravy. Then the rest was mashed and divided and served on a piece of bread. We folded the bread round it and ate it as a sandwich. It tasted delicious. That was what we often ate as our main meal of the day — sometimes for days on end. We used to eat with our hands. We washed our hands and sat round the *korsi* where the food was served, and shared a bowl between two or three of us. Afterwards a bowl of warm water would be brought around for us to wash our hands. The bowls were all copper. The slow-cooking dishes were earthenware or heavy pottery. For a special treat we had rice with noodles and a drop of oil with the stew, once a month or every six weeks if we could afford it. Mother made the noodles from flour. Most days we ate food such as yoghurt with bread, cheese with bread and onion, strained yoghurt, soups, in winter lots of thick soups, with pulses, noodles, and lots of dried herbs and spices. It smelled good, tasted good, maybe because we were very hungry. A lot of bread was eaten. Whenever we were hungry we would have some bread. Bread was cooked in large flat thin loaves fresh every day or every other day. Mother baked. It smelled beautiful and tasted delicious. Sometimes we had some cheese with it or yoghurt. In summer we drank diluted yoghurt into which we put pieces of bread, chopped cucumber, spring onions and garlic.

I played out in the street a lot with other children. I mixed well. I was accepted. I never felt that I was different from them. I did more or less what other children did, boys and girls.

One summer night as we were sleeping on the roof, when father was away, mother woke up in the middle of the night and saw a strange man standing beside her. 'Oh! Hello.' Then she recognized him as an old acquaintance to whom father owed money. People often borrowed from each other, paying back when they could.

This man seemed secretive and devious. Mother didn't like the look of him. 'Oh, you've come for your money?' she said quickly and got up straightaway but when she turned he went off. She woke us and the neighbours and four or five men took sticks and bricks and went to the woods nearby to look for him. But they didn't find anyone and after a while came back. Mother was cross with father for having dealings with a man like that and for putting her and the family in danger. The intruder was never heard of or seen again.

Mother usually felt secure in the neighbourhood. People looked after one another and women chatted any time of the day. That was how they kept going under those conditions. They were in and out of each other's houses all the time. They gave each other practical help. If mother wasn't well, we were never left unattended. Our food was cooked, clothes washed and the house cleaned. Men helped each other as well. If father wasn't well and it was a severe winter day, a neighbour would sweep the snow away from the roof and out of the yard. People might have been hungry but there was no isolation or insecurity. The landlords were unjust but people helped each other and looked after each other. People were together a lot. Togetherness was characteristic of that community. Women did their washing together. They chose a day, and took their washing to the stream nearby. They did their washing there on the large stones, and talked as they worked. Loneliness was not known. They fetched water together. Every evening mother would take the *kuzeh*, a tall pottery container with a narrow top and a handle, to the centre of the village to fetch water from the well or to the spring where the water was clean, fresh and cool. The young girls sang as they carried the water, and recited poems and told stories in the cool summer evening as they walked along in their colourful clothes. On winter nights they visited each other after dinner. Families went to each other's houses and spent a few hours together. They talked, the women helped with the carpet weaving and they ate some dried fruit and melon or pumpkin seeds which had been dried and roasted.

We spun wool. After the sheep had been sheared the wool was washed and dried in the sun. I had a little spindle, a small stick that was fitted into a wheel over which I stretched the wool. I took a little wool at a time until it was like a string and then twisted it round using the spindle and wound the wool on to the stick and started again. When the stick was full, I would take it out and start again. We wound the finished wool into loops using our knees or someone's arms stretched out. When all the loops were ready they weighed about two or three pounds each and mother would dye them. After that we unwound the loops into balls. All this wool went to the landlord because the sheep belonged to him. I couldn't understand why it was that mother milked all the time but we never received any. The same with the cheese and yoghurt and oil which we made in our house, and the wool which was cut and processed and dyed and woven into carpets which we never sat on. I didn't understand. It all went to the landlord.

Mother and father prayed three times a day, in the morning before sunrise, in the afternoon before sunset, and evening prayer after sunset. At evening prayer the family problems were expressed. Mother always asked God to bless her children (the boys were prayed for first), to provide a livelihood for them, to give her strength to carry on and to preserve her health and the children's health. She prayed for each of us separately. I would hold my breath and listen intently to hear whether my name would come up. Then, though sometimes spoken half-heartedly and with hesitation, I would hear my name. God, ... Monir; then she would go silent for a minute or two — or murmur to herself something that I did not understand. I never understood what mother prayed for me for. I didn't seem to count. I was always disappointed when mother prayed. Evening prayers would take fifteen to twenty minutes. For mother prayer was a meditation, a release from the day's worries, anxieties and burdens, from her fear of the landlord, and of her husband.

CHAPTER FIVE

The time had come when we could no longer stay in the village. We were in debt. Father had borrowed grain for us to make bread and the debt accumulated. It was time to make a decision. We didn't have anything to sell to raise money so we had to move away. Go to Teheran. There were stories about Teheran, the capital. It would be an easy life there, we heard, everyone can find work, even me. Yes, there would be work for a little girl like me. Even a blind girl could find work, could earn a living. I could swing a baby to sleep in a cradle and earn a living as easy as that. Father said we shouldn't waste time. We should prepare ourselves to move and we should keep quiet about it. No word to anyone, apart from immediate family. My uncle was told and my aunts, Aunt Zolikha and Aunt Asli, and their husbands. No word to anyone else. No one in the village should know we are moving otherwise word would get to the landlord and then we would be in trouble. Father went to see the shopkeeper in the village, who trusted him and respected him. He agreed to keep our belongings and give us some money for travelling. The idea was that we would move to Teheran, find ourselves a house and work and save enough to return for our belongings and to pay the landlord. All our valuables — the copper bowls, the *aftabeh*, the large copper tray Akbar and I had once lost in the river; the heavy copper saucepan which mother made rice in occasionally as a special treat; the large quilt which we put over the *korsi* for everyone to sleep under in winter, an old rug and the brass samovar and a few other bits and pieces — were all put in mother's large trunk, locked up and taken to the shopkeeper's house as deposit. He gave us about 1,875 rial which we could use for travelling. Father had hired two donkeys. These would take us to Dameh the nearest town. From there we could hire two other donkeys to take us to Ghazvin a bigger town, and from there we could travel by lorry. It was all very exciting but we had to keep very quiet, mouths sealed, and we had to set off in the middle of the night when the village was asleep.

We were woken in the middle of the night. My aunts were there to say goodbye. Silence and whispering. We shouldn't take the lamp out into the yard, someone might see a light and suspect. Everything was ready. We started off. Aunt Zolikha held a Koran over us at the gate and as we passed through she threw water behind us. A custom that offered protection for our return. But we were not to return. She was crying quietly. My mother and father kissed the aunts and said goodbye, and they kissed us all and Aunt Zolikha kept saying she hoped she would see us soon.

We set off on the two donkeys. We took lightweight clothes with us and our aunts had given us some bread and a few boiled eggs to have on the journey, and some cheese. Father walked. My brothers and my mother holding my little baby sister of eight or nine months old, and our belongings were on the donkeys. We had to get out of the village as soon as possible and with the minimum of noise. My father kept on repeating, 'In God's name, in the name of God, let no one see us, may God protect us and see us through this journey.' My mother was quiet and I'm sure she was praying too. Maybe this was one of the few moments they were in agreement together. It was a crisis, a turning point in their lives. We felt secure. They were together, agreeing together, in silence except for father's whispered words. I fell asleep soon, and did not know anything else until the following morning. I woke. We were still travelling and father was still walking. We must stop at some point and have a rest, and give the donkeys a rest, father said. 'Poor animals. All this weight, and all this way, and they haven't had a drink.' He found them a drink and we had a rest and some bread to eat, and some water to drink. It was in the country. Nobody around. Nobody passing. No sign of life anywhere. Soon we started again. Father was anxious that we should get as far away as we could from the village. It wasn't safe to be anywhere near it. We set off.

We travelled most of that day and arrived in Dameh towards evening. Father found a guest house for the night and next day we picked up two more donkeys to take us to Ghazvin.

When we arrived in Ghazvin I could hear the roar of traffic there. Huge vehicles, lorries making a big noise over the dusty rough roads. It was frightening. So many people, so much noise. This was amazing, bewildering. 'It's so busy here,' mother said, 'so many people around, so much noise.' 'You wait until you see Teheran,' father said, laughing. 'You don't know what Teheran is like.' Father had been to Teheran before. He had even been to Rasht on the Caspian Sea further than Teheran to look for work, but he hadn't found anything useful or permanent. But this was going to be different. He was going to make his fortune. Taking the family, it is different. He couldn't concentrate, he said, on his own. He was worried about his family all the time. This had long been his plan — that he would take his family with him and make his fortune in Teheran. And now mother's family had moved there — Ahmad, mother's middle brother was working there in a café. A café. Imagine that. He must be very well off. Ahmad would help father and mother. We would soon find work. No doubt about it. He was certain that there was work waiting for me. I would start straight away, swinging a baby to sleep in a *nanou*, in a cradle. Imagine that. I could do that quite easily. What does it involve? Just sitting there and swinging the baby to sleep with one hand. That was easy enough. Children always helped mothers swing the baby to sleep. And that was very valuable in Teheran. There were lots of rich people who would have a girl come and swing their babies to sleep. Their own children wouldn't do such a thing, they were too well off, they were ladies and lords, how could they be expected to swing a baby to sleep, but I could. They wouldn't mind my doing it, mother and father wouldn't mind, and I wouldn't mind doing it, and I would earn my own living. How about that? So they wouldn't have to worry about me, that would feed me all right.

We had to wait to return the donkeys and father had to arrange for a lorry to take us to Teheran. It would be very exciting, to sit in a lorry. Lots of other people were waiting too, with their belongings, all on the side of the road. After some time we were told we had to wait the night there, the lorry wasn't leaving until next day. Here we had to find a travellers' house. We found one. There was one large hall for women, one for men. That night we all huddled together in this smelly room, next to each other, and next to us many, many other women and children slept. They were all smelly and the children sometimes cried. I felt mother hadn't slept at all with the worry and the noise, but we slept. In the morning we had to be ready early. The lorry was leaving. We all got on to the lorry. I was picked up by father and put inside the lorry. Father had to bargain with the driver to take us. We didn't have enough money but we had to get to Teheran, we couldn't be left stranded in Ghazvin. Eventually the driver agreed to take us and father was grateful. We started off. It was very bumpy. It hurt our bums. Mother said her bum was hurting too. The lorry was packed with people. I couldn't move my legs easily to change my sitting position, and children were crying. There was a kind of misery in the air, uncertainty, anxiety, strangeness. Everyone was a stranger to everyone else. We weren't used to being with strangers, or to meeting them. People felt reticent. Children cried. I didn't cry. I just sat there. I was used to silence, to being quiet. I just sat there. People would forget I was there sometimes because I did not make any noise or complain. I was no trouble. The lorry kept moving on, bumpy, jerky, dusty, very uncomfortable, shaking us all the time and suddenly going down steep hills and up again and we felt as though we would all drop off the truck any minute. And it was hot, the sun on our heads. Eventually we reached Abgram where we had to stop for lunch. *Ab* is water, *gram* is warm, warm waters, in other words there were hot underground springs there. People visited Abgram from all over believing that the hot baths cured all sorts of illnesses. Now we had a chance to visit the baths, everyone wanted the chance of having a bath in those waters. We went to a coffee house. The driver ordered *abgusht*. They served *abgusht* in small individual pots and my brother Ali looked at the driver so hungrily that he offered him some. My father told us about it. The driver was such a generous man, he offered food to this child, see how kind people can be. In the afternoon we went bathing in the underground baths. It was salty, warm, nice. We stayed in Abgram overnight again and next day the same lorry would take us to Teheran. I do not remember much about the journey between Abgram and Teheran. Maybe I slept the whole way. Maybe I sensed we were approaching the land of my sufferings. I escaped to sleep. We arrived in Teheran.

We were left dumped in this wasteland. I remember there were a couple of other families with us on that waste ground which was at the back of some houses. The people living in the houses had thrown their rubbish out on to the ground and my mother and the other ladies looked through the rubbish and they found a toothbrush. They saw this toothbrush and they didn't know what it was. What is it for? They kept talking about how rich people were. Look what kind of things they throw away. We are lucky to have come here. We are going to make our fortune. This is going to be the end of our sufferings, thank God. God is great, they kept saying. I touched the toothbrushes they were talking about. I wanted to know everything, everything they talked about. I would bide my time until I could somehow get hold of the thing and touch it, to know what it was. I would wait until the time was right to search for it, to ask for it.

We had to find my mother's family, who knew we were coming. But it would take time. I remember standing at the roadside and hearing these cars going past one way and then the other, one way and then the other, coming and going. I couldn't understand how there could be so many cars in the world, all the time I was waiting there, all those different cars. Surely there couldn't be so many cars in the world. I decided there must be only two or three, going first in one direction and then returning from the other. That's it. But I couldn't understand the purpose of doing this. I just stood there in amazement. Maybe they're just driving to show off, I thought. In the past when a car came to the village, which only happened once or twice a year, everyone went out to look at it. That's it. They're just going round and round for people to see, like us, that must be it. But they came so quickly I thought, it's clever. My young mind could not imagine there would be so many cars in Teheran. It seemed to be magic. And the roads, all smooth and even. It wasn't hilly and bumpy, up and down, sharp stones as in the village. The footpaths were beautifully straight and even, I could run along them. Mother couldn't stop talking about what kind of things she could see in the wasteland. Empty tins, broken combs. That comb that she found wasn't much broken. Just a few teeth, that's all. It was dirty all right, but she could give it a wash. It was an unusual comb. It wasn't wooden, like her wooden comb. It was made out of something different. Father said it was plastic. What does this mean, mother said. Anyway it's very different from ours. It must be very nice. Nice colour. She was excited. She couldn't wait to meet her family. I wonder what kind of things they have, she kept wondering. In this wasteland. People from the houses were looking at us from their windows. We found some bits of dried bread somewhere. They were laughing at us, mother said, but she wasn't offended.

Eventually we found a room in a house. The lady of the house worked in the hospital. She used to wear high heels in the morning when she went out. I loved to listen to her high-heeled shoes taking small small steps, walking fast. Mother found her family, and mother used to leave me at home and go and visit them. All by myself, I would stay home all day. There was some bread, mother would say, and when you are hungry have some bread. I used to feel so miserable, left out, abandoned. I wasn't part of the family. My brothers and my baby sister would go with her but I would be left behind; it would break my heart. I used to cry, in this house, all on my own. Father used to go out looking for work, of course, all day and mother quite often visited my uncles. When they came back the other children, especially my brothers, would have been given presents, and sometimes mother would say this coin is for you but I'm keeping it for you. But I knew she was making it up, they hadn't given me anything. I felt very sad, heartbroken. When she did take me with her occasionally I felt left out because I did not understand the language. Mother spoke Kurdish with her family. I did not know Kurdish. I spoke Turkish, my father's language. So I felt totally left out.

I used to hear mother talking about all sorts of wonders with the neighbour. They used to watch through the window. They saw a lorry emptying bricks. They saw it lift up, higher and higher, and empty all the bricks by itself. They couldn't see anyone lifting it up. And then again, all by itself, it would gradually come down. Wasn't that amazing? It was magic. How could that happen? They could see many things in Teheran with their own eyes which if they'd heard described they would not have believed. Seeing with their own eyes such things happening in Teheran. 'We must show so and so,' they would say and they would talk about it with such excitement. 'You have to see it for yourself,' they would say to the next friend. 'It really does happen and there is no one to lift the thing up. It couldn't be lifted up by a hundred men, it just goes up by itself and empties the stuff out, all those bricks, tons of them, and then it just comes down by itself. Who would have thought I could experience such things in life, see such things.'

'It's with the press of a button or a lever somewhere,' father would say, 'the driver's doing it.' Even then mother would exclaim, 'How can it be?'

'Well, you wait and see, there are other, much more amazing things in Teheran, you haven't seen anything yet,' father would say with amusement.

'More amazing than this, I don't believe it.'

CHAPTER SIX

Mother was happy now, full of life and energy being near her family and seeing such amazing things around her, new things. It all fascinated her and she enjoyed it.

Gradually, father became disillusioned, disheartened. He couldn't find work, not permanent and well paid, as he expected and hoped. He could do little bits and pieces here and there, now and then, such as emptying and cleaning out the ponds in people's gardens. He would take two large buckets and walk the streets calling out *Ab hose keshi* (pond cleaner), so people who wanted their ponds emptied and cleaned would come out and take him on. When the job was finished — maybe it would take a couple of hours — they would give him something, occasionally a little money, and that was it, and he would carry on walking and calling out again. He'd go for days without any work; nevertheless he would walk around, which was how he got to know Teheran very well. There were too many like him on the market: at times two or three others would pass him on the same street, so there was not much chance of work.

Many people came from the villages to Teheran looking for work. Some lived by the side of the road. They didn't have a roof over their heads. We were the lucky ones. We had some relations there, who had found us accommodation, and we were eating better than when we were in the village, with the help of my mother's family, my uncles and grandmother.

Grandmother disliked me instantly. She was horrid to me. She always spoke harshly to me. From her I got the message, what are you doing here, we could have done without you. I was frightened of her. Mother rarely took me there. I was always left at home on my own, unless it was a special occasion or my mother wanted to stay overnight and father wasn't sure when he'd get back. Sometimes I just went to sleep when I was left alone. It broke my heart, thinking I had left my beloved Aunt Zolikha behind and come to this horrid grandmother.

Mother was ashamed of me. She felt inadequate with me around, especially in front of her own mother. I was an embarrassment. She wished somehow I would disappear off the face of the earth. I was a disgrace. Maybe she felt guilty, and that she should have prevented my blindness, should not have given birth to me. And now that I was there, she didn't quite know what to do with me. If only I would disappear. If she could do magic, put a spell on me, she would.

Once she tried to dispose of me. I must have been five or six years old. We had a long way to go that day. She had gone for a job, and had not succeeded in getting it; she was disappointed, grumpy, tired. It was a hot day, a long way to walk. A wasted journey.

She grumbled, muttered, cursing me as we walked. The streets were quiet. We were passing the gardens. I could hear the trees, the wind rustling the leaves. The gardens stretched for a long way. Nobody about. Where had all the people gone? I asked myself. Nobody lives in these houses. Where are they? I felt insecure not hearing anyone around. It was the rich part of the town, with big houses and large gardens and few people. There were always lots of people about where we lived.

I was walking on her left, holding on to her, quietly. I did not dare say anything; it was too dangerous to say anything; worried; anxious; listening out for any human sound. She kept blaming me, cursing 'You are a headache. You are a nuisance. What do you want from me? Why don't you leave me alone? Why don't you just go and leave me free,' as she put it.

I felt alarmed, frightened. Especially with nobody around. Would anyone walk by? Was there any sign of life anywhere? I kept listening hard. She wished I would disappear, simply disappear. But where to, I thought to myself? How? But I am here,

I am alive. I pinched myself to make sure I could feel it, the pain, that I existed. It was an autumn day, the sun was shining, there was a nice breeze.

We came to a hole in the ground on my side of the pavement near the wall. I sensed it as we approached. She pushed me towards it, pulling me, pushing me somehow, towards this hole. She wanted to throw me in it. I held on to her arm, held on to her chador tightly. She pushed my hand off her arm. I held on to her trodor with both hands tight and stood there as firmly as I could, panic stricken. We had stopped. I had felt her strong wish to get rid of me. I felt her willingness to get rid of me.

I kept silent. It was too dangerous. I had to breathe quietly. 'What now?' I said to myself, as we stood there. She kept muttering that she had had enough of me, that she wished I didn't exist. What did I want from her? Why didn't I leave her alone? She gave a push. I felt my heart beat. I held my breath. I felt the ground underneath my feet as though they were stuck to it. Nothing could move them. I was nailed there. I stood there silent.

I had to be silent at danger points if I wanted to survive. I had learned this very early on. Could not show how fearful and hopeless I felt. I did not scream, hit her, call her names. 'It's not my fault what you are going through, you wretched woman.'

Gradually, mother started moving, still muttering, cursing, and I moved with her. We passed people's gardens, they seemed to stretch for miles. All this space, all these gardens, no people in them, I kept wondering. The emptiness I felt in the space, was it my own emptiness of human touch, concern and care? All these gardens exist without people, what for then?

The whole way I clung to her and dragged myself behind her. Not a word of complaint. I did not feel tired or thirsty. I could not afford this. I felt grateful when we got home still alive. I had to keep going all the time in silence.

My mother took me to my uncle's wedding. There was a room for the women guests and another for the men. My mother took me because she could not leave me anywhere, but she would rather not have taken me. But I was there. Amd she sat me in a corner in the room and said, 'Sit there, and don't move.' Gradually, visitors started to come and the room became full. I just sat in that corner for a long time. Nobody talked to me. I was tiny. Perhaps nobody noticed me.

The room was absolutely packed and the party was in full swing. I suddenly decided this was enough. I was not going to sit in that corner forever, all on my own, isolated in that crowded room. So I got up and bit by bit walked towards the front. People were sitting side by side on the floor. Women in their pretty dresses. The room was packed and they were handing tea and sweets to each other. I kept pushing and stepping over people's legs and chadors, and moving towards the front of the room. It was a very large room, there were hundreds of guests, packed close together in many rows.

After a while people began to notice me and to help me along. Eventually I reached the front, and sat there, in front of everybody. Mother came along. She was furious with me. In a quiet voice she told me off. 'You stepped over everyone and got here!' Her tone was sharp, biting, vicious. I did not answer. Then I was given some sweets and made to sit down.

I was so belittled, brushed aside, in Teheran, and what's more I hadn't found a job. Not a baby in a cradle to swing so I could earn my living. I felt I'd failed. I'd failed my parents as well. My brother hadn't found anything either. They had hoped he would go into some kind of apprenticeship, learn to be something, a carpenter or a tailor, learn some skill to earn his living and hopefully in future to support our parents, the family, as well. He was only about eight or nine years old.

Father tried anything, anything that was suggested to him or he could think of. He tried construction work. He went every morning and stood in a queue on the roadside at a designated spot where the workers would be selected. Say an employer wanted ten labourers, and there would be maybe fifty in the queue, they would choose ten men who looked the strongest and my father was never chosen because he did not look strong and he was not tall or heavily built. He gave up that idea. I remember his return every day after he had queued a few hours in the strong sun. Mother would be heartbroken. I could feel her deep sense of rejection and hopelessness. His body had failed him. He was no good, he was a frail, fragile, delicate looking man. I felt he would have liked to have used his mind, if he had the chance, rather than his body. Maybe he would have made a good academic. He was honest, straightforward, sensitive. He was bright, imaginative. He would take risks. He would try anything. Sometimes he would say things in a temper such as, 'In this world you have to be a crook to succeed, and I am not.' My father's decline started there and then, bit by bit. He became more disheartened, more disappointed. Sometimes he would come home with a bundle of dried bread which he'd received in exchange for some work in a house or for emptying a pond. We would soak the bread and then put some soup or something on it and eat it. Quite often he would come home empty-handed and then he was silent and wouldn't talk to anyone, I think he was ashamed. Sometimes we used to have raisins or peanuts that mother kept for emergencies, and sometimes we ate just dried bread dipped in water. My father felt especially inadequate in front of mother's family. He had a strong sense of failure. One of my uncles, Uncle Ahmad, the one working in a café, had a house with two rooms in it. I remember it had a small yard. Eight or nine of them lived there. Relatives would come and go all the time, and stay with them. Sometimes during the day the house was absolutely packed. People came from villages all the time to stay overnight or for a day. Father decided we had to move to try to find work for him. He wanted to get away from my mother's family who didn't really like him. They didn't feel comfortable with him. Father felt uncomfortable with them and very unhappy, having been uprooted, having left his family behind in Kahleh. He did not speak Farsi, which was the language spoken in Teheran, and he felt very out of place, a foreigner. He was a Turk from the Turkish minority in Iran and my mother was Kurd, from the Kurdish minority. The majority of the population spoke Farsi. The Turks were regarded as a stupid race. Many jokes went round about them, about how they were like donkeys, they were thick. So my father quite often had a hostile reception.

Eventually he found a place for us in the upper part of the town. It was still a working-class area. He'd got to know someone there who managed a garage, a depot where repairs were also carried out, and who needed someone to look after it, so father took the job. There was a shop with a basement room where we could live next door to the garage. We moved in. The garage manager was called Mashhadi Akbar, which suggested he'd visited Mashad, the holy city in Iran. Whether or not he actually had visited Mashad we did not know.

Lots of cars and lorries drove in to the garage and parked for a short time, and sometimes father had to get up in the middle of the night and open the garage doors for people to drive in or out. On summer nights we slept in the garage forecourt in the open air. We would close the gates and lay the bedding out on the ground and sleep there. One night we all had to get up and pick up our bed rolls because the owner of the garage had arrived. Father said the garage owner, who was a young man, was a very nice person. He talked to father and treated him politely, so father had a lot of respect for him. Occasionally the owner gave father a tip of some sort as he chatted to him. He was a very well spoken and modest man, father thought.

Father wasn't earning much at the garage and mother started work as a washerwoman. She used to go to houses and wash people's clothes and receive something in exchange — sometimes a couple of kilos of rice, or sugar, or a little money, or something like that which she would bring home. She would leave in the early morning, and return home for lunch at about one or two o'clock. She would normally bring home whatever lunch they had given her and share it with us. The middle class could afford to have a washerwoman once or twice a week to wash their clothes and sheets, and so mother would go early morning and sometimes wouldn't come home until evening. The whole day, she had to work. Some households also had a maid, a young girl who lived in to help the lady in the house. I used to go with my mother sometimes. This was to the friendly households, the ones who were mother's favourite customers.

Mother would use a large round cast iron bowl. First she rinsed the clothes with cold water and then she poured hot water into the bowl and washed the clothes one by one, using her hands and a bar of soap. She would squat, usually in the garden and just wash away, rubbing one by one till everything was clean. She would wash once, and change the water, and wash a second time. Then she would rinse the clothes three times in clear water, still using the cast-iron bowl, and when all the suds had been rinsed out she gave everything a final rinse in the *hose* (garden pond). Every household had a pond with a fountain in the middle. It was these ponds father used to clean. People changed the pond water once a week so the clothes were finally rinsed in this pond for complete cleanliness and then the white ones were rinsed once more with a whitener in the bowl and hung up. It was very hard work. It could take anything from four to six hours, depending on the amount of washing to be done. People preferred having mother visit twice a week, so she would work for five hours non-stop. All winter as well she would do the washing out in the garden, in the freezing cold. My mother would just squat there in the yard and wash away. Occasionally the family let her do the washing in the bathroom. 'That was a great treat, they were wonderful conditions,' she thought, being allowed to use as much hot water as she liked. Sometimes she rinsed the clothes in warm water. In winter this was wonderful. She talked about how generous and kind those people were letting her use the bathroom and as much hot water as she needed. She used to bring home old clothes and things for herself and for us, given to her by those ladies.

She had one favourite lady, who was Jewish. The common

prejudice was, at that time, that Jews were stringent, mean and dirty, so people usually kept away from them, but mother thought this woman was completely the opposite. 'She's cleaner than all these Muslims who claim to be Muslims,' she went on, 'she's not stringent or mean at all. She gives me a generous lunch. She knows I'm sharing it with my children. And what's more,' she went on, 'when she gives me food she covers it. I don't understand why, when I carry it out she covers it for me. I wonder why.' She didn't realize her employer might think that mother might be embarrassed. She could not imagine anyone having that much concern for her. She was very happy with that family. The lady was kind, she treated her with dignity, decency, she was human. 'Much better than some of the Muslim women,' mother would go on about it. 'Some of these so-called Muslims,' she would say, 'some of them would give me tiny little bits of leftovers for lunch but the Jewish lady, no, she would give me a nice lot right from the pot.' She knew mother would share it with us. Mother said: 'she would say she was serving mine. Then she takes the food out of the pot, a great big plateful, more than she would serve for herself, and puts mine away until I am ready to go. Then puts it on a tray and covers the tray with a cloth.' Mother could not get over this. She even covers the tray with a cloth. She would look forward to that every week. She would go there with enthusiasm and once a week we would get a good meal. Normally it was rice with some stew. We would have it with bread and divide this plate amongst five of us, mother, father, my two brothers and me. The baby, my sister, who was a year old now, was almost not counted. She was just left at home. I used to hear my mother saying, 'Oh, don't suck it, I haven't got any milk, let it go. When she sucks it makes me feel horrible.' So the baby would go hungry, for long periods. I used to think, Well, what can she eat then? and a sense of despair would fill me. She didn't cry either. I don't remember her cries, she was just like me. She just lay there. She just slept. Somehow, I don't know how, she kept going, alive.

The day father took me to the street to beg it was a summer's day, it was early morning and I didn't know what was happening. Father asked me to go with him. I was surprised. So early in the morning, I'd just woken up. Where was he taking me? We climbed the stairs together. He held my right hand. We turned right at the top of the street. It was a busy road, the traffic was roaring, the sun was shining. I didn't know where we were going. We walked a little longer until we were at the traffic lights where we crossed to the left. Father had been quiet up to this time and so had I. I was always quiet. Then he said, 'You come and sit here. There,' he sat me on the corner of this busy junction next to the wall. 'Sit properly,' he said. I sat cross-legged. 'That's better,' he said. Then father took my right hand and rested it on my left leg. 'Keep this hand open, here. People will drop coins into it.' He gave me a little cloth bag. 'Put the money in this bag and hold it with your other hand. Hold it tight won't you? I'll come and see you soon.'

He was awkward. His voice was tremulous. His hand shook as he opened my hand over my lap and before I had a chance to say anything he had disappeared. He had left me there. I was abandoned, lost, forgotten. I felt cut off from my family, from everyone I knew. I was on this strange, busy, bewildering corner. How could I make contact with them again? I thought to myself, 'I can't. I've lost touch with them forever.' I could have screamed. 'Come back father, don't leave me here, stay with me, take me home, stay with me, be with me, someone be with me, someone I know, don't leave me here.' I could hear my heart beating. All this had happened so suddenly, so dramatically. For a moment it seemed like a dream, I thought this was only just a bad dream, I would wake in a minute and everything would be over. I kept pinching myself to wake up. Coins kept dropping into my hand as people passed by. 'In the name of God,' they said as they passed. They were mostly men on their way to work. It was rush hour, a stream of people going by in every direction. It was such a crowd, such a rush, traffic roaring. What if they step over me? I was frightened of being stepped over, squashed, crumpled under their feet. Fear, bewilderment, abandonment filled me, shook me, smashed me like a piece of glass.

Eventually things quietened down, not so many people passed by, not so many coins were dropped into my hand. My money bag was full up, my hand was full as well. Then suddenly a big surprise — Father came to take the money. He emptied the bag, took all the money from my hand, and gave me the empty bag, and said he'd come and take me home for lunch, and he left straight away. He came back at lunchtime. After lunch I was taken there again. This was repeated every day. I got more money in the morning, early morning, and in the evening, when people were going to and from work, the rush hours.

I was given a money box made of pottery, a big one. 'This is for you,' Mother said, 'you can put your money in it, and it will be all yours.' I was thrilled. I took the money box and put all the money in it. It was quite heavy with the coins. This is great, I felt. It was all mine. Mine only. My brother didn't have a money box. This was wonderful. So every day I went to the corner with enthusiasm. I would save all my money and put it in my money box, I said to myself. One day when I went home and wanted to put my money into the box mother said to me, 'Look let me hold it today. You put the money in.' 'But why? I want to hold it myself.' 'No, look people will see. I'd better hold it today,' mother said. I wasn't convinced of that. I was used to holding my money box while I put the money in. What was different today? I didn't argue. I put the coins in as she showed me, so I didn't actually touch the money box and mother put it away. 'I'll hide it quickly,' she said, 'so that nobody will see it.' Next day she said the same thing, but I insisted that I wanted to have my money box. I wanted to hold it. Mother gave it to me. This was strange. There was a cloth wrapped round it, like a bandage. 'Why is this?' I asked. 'Oh, well, er, I didn't want people to see what is in there you see,' mother explained. It didn't feel so heavy, not heavy at all. 'All those coins I've been putting in, it should be much heavier than this,' I said to

myself. I shook it. I learned the painful truth. It had been cracked, broken, and the pieces put together again and bandaged for me. Mother had taken money out of it to buy things like a kettle or a saucepan. I felt shattered, smashed, broken just like the money box. My trust had been betrayed. I'd been deceived. My treasure had been broken into, stolen, I cried bitterly. For a long time whenever mother spoke of it to anyone I begged her to stop. The pain of it was too much for me to bear. The hurt was too much. My money box had been my secret. My treasure, something of my own, the only thing I had ever had all to myself. The money was to be used for myself, only me. I would buy nice things with it, new clothes, maybe dolls, something nice for me, just me. My secret had been stolen from me. My treasure.

I felt I'd been used, misused, I'd been put to beg without anyone asking me whether I wanted to do it. I wasn't asked. I was put out to beg. No one explained to me what was going to happen. I was put there against my will. I was used like an object, then I was given this money box and told it was my own, and anything I made from begging would go in it. It would be my own, only mine, and I'd trusted that, and now that trust had been betrayed. I'd been deceived. My money had been taken. I didn't care about the money after that. I gave it all to them. It didn't mean anything to me any longer. They can use all of it now, I thought, my secret's gone, my treasure's gone. That money was mine, those coins, people had given them to me, not to them. The unfairness and injustice of this filled me deeply. It hurt. The money box had a very special significance to me. The only wealth I'd ever had, and my wealth gave me worth. My secret had a very special meaning. I valued it highly and now all my hopes were shattered. I used to hold the money box in my arms like a baby. And they used to put the coins in one by one with great care, and then I would lift it and feel the heaviness. That would give me joy. See how heavy it is, how much money I have in here. I regarded it just like a baby, my own baby.

The government considered that all these beggars on the street corners of Teheran were too unsightly. We were told policemen went round every afternoon in lorries and picked them up. Though, the beggars who had enough money to bribe the authorities would be released and start again. This was all new to us. But I suppose that, somehow, we were expecting it when, one day, a vehicle stopped, a man picked me up, and put me in a lorry. There were lots of other people there. 'Where are you taking me?' I asked.

'Don't worry, we're taking you to the Beggars' House,' I was told. I sat on the floor. I played with the policeman's shoelaces while others talked to him. One man offered 1,250 rial. He was bargaining for his release. My father would not have that kind of money to give for me, I thought. This was the end then, I never would see them again. How would they find me? They would not find me. I would never see them. But I kept quiet, silent. I did not cry. I did not scream. I did not complain. I kept playing with the policeman's shoelaces. The van or lorry was driving along the streets. We went on and on and on. The further we went the more anxious I became. I was going far from my family. The hope of their ever finding me was fading, it would be impossible, it was too far. Nobody could walk all this distance, I thought. My mother couldn't walk all this distance, nor my father, so they couldn't find me. They couldn't walk all this distance. This is it. I will never see them again. I felt the same as on the first day my father had put me out there on that corner, that busy junction, and left me. I'd felt abandoned, and the same feeling came to me now – abandoned, lost, this is it, I am lost now, I am truly lost now, abandoned, forgotten. The lorry was full of strangers, older men, mostly men, or old women. I was the only child. After a drive that lasted an eternity, we arrived at Amirabad, a long way out of town.

I fell ill soon afterwards. It was quite a severe illness. I never knew what that illness was. For some time I did not know anything. I do not remember anything. Just as with my smallpox I do not remember anything. Maybe weeks or months passed. Gradually I gained consciousness. I felt very weak. I would just lie there for hours on end. People would lift me up and carry me to the toilet — or if I did walk I was very weak. I couldn't take more than a few steps at a time and then I had to sit down. Once when I was trying to walk to the toilet — I had only a vague idea of where to go — I couldn't get there. I kept sitting down. One of the guards, a young man, asked me where I wanted to go. I explained and he said come on, take the end of the stick and follow me. So I held the end of the stick and he led me to the toilet, and when I finished and came out, I held the end of his stick again and he took me back to where I was supposed to be. On another occasion another young man put me on his shoulders and he chatted to me. I think he was on national service, and he was looking forward to going home in a few days. He talked to me. I found this surprising — that a man talked to me on an equal level and actually treated me decently. I felt so good. He was a cheerful, happy, kind person, and he told me how he was looking forward to returning to his family. His tone of voice and the ride on his shoulder — he made me feel good by just talking to me.

It was a very crowded place. There was a large hall full of women and girls. I was the youngest child there. The men had another hall, or two other halls. It was very big. The authorities would come round, now and then, to check whether we had our crockery, our bowls. I put mine out for them to see just as the others did. I had a little cupboard to keep my things in, and I was told to take everything out for inspection.

One day they came to take me to the office. 'Your mother's come to see you,' they said. Mother? My mother? I couldn't believe it. She'd found me. I went in. Yes, mother was there. I was going home with mother and we were going to walk back. All that way. She was unhappy, tired. She had walked all the way there. The thought of walking all the way back with me was too much for her. We started off. We walked and walked and walked. Couldn't we get the *doreshkeh* (horse-drawn carriage) I would say occasionally, sitting down to rest. 'No, I haven't got the money,' she would say, 'we have to walk.' Sometimes we stopped and asked a shopkeeper for a drink of water. Eventually, we got home. Immediately I collapsed. I fell asleep. I slept for a very long time. Later mother told the others that I slept and slept and slept. 'I just let her sleep.' Later mother changed me, and washed me and cut my hair. I had lice everywhere. I lay in bed for a long time. I was too weak to get up, or maybe too depressed. It took me a long time to recover.

I felt my mother only came to fetch me because of the way people were talking. It was social pressure rather than genuine personal concern. What people thought mattered most. I felt more of a burden. It was as though she was saying, 'I have to cope with you now you are here. I can't ignore other people's attitudes. I would be ostracized. I can't take that. I have to put up with you, you're like a mill-stone round my neck. Why couldn't I forget about you and leave you there? You weren't around for a couple of months — it was better. Why didn't you die there? What a grip on life you have.' She would often say this. 'She's got such a grip on life.'

While I was away, my baby sister had died aged one-and-a-half. 'Where's Khanomtaj?' I asked, when I came to. 'She died,' mother said. 'She was ill.' Died? Was it because I went away? I wasn't around to look after her. I wasn't bringing money in. She was always hungry. I remember her faint voice. 'Ah, ah, ah,' she would go on. She didn't have energy to say it louder, to demand food. She had died of hunger. She never cried. She just lay there, just as I had when I was a baby. She had demanded just enough to keep her alive, just as I had. 'It's a relief,' mother would say, 'all that suffering.' I felt responsible for her death in some way. If I had been there when mother left to go to work, I would have looked after her. Or mother wouldn't have been so worried about me and would have given her something to help her live. It was certainly my responsibility. These thoughts went through my mind for a long time. I was sadder, heavier, but I did not cry. I remembered the moments when I used to hold my sister and carry her around. She was so docile, passive, no trouble, and yet

she'd died of hunger. She'd starved to death, literally, she had starved to death, my poor sister. My poor darling sister.

One night I had a fantasy that mother, wondering whether I may have been sexually abused at the Beggars' House, checked me in my sleep. I was all right. It was a miracle. Miracles do happen. They happened for me. It was a miracle that I did not die in the Beggars' House, it was a miracle that I did not die when I had the smallpox, and it was a miracle that I had not been sexually abused. I had a feeling that somehow I had been looked after by some power, some force, somewhere. I wasn't put out to beg on the street after that.

CHAPTER SEVEN

Ali often beat up our younger brother Akbar. He used to burn Akbar's feet with a long iron bar. He used to heat the bar on the stove and then corner Akbar in the room. I remember Akbar's screams and distress. We were frightened of Ali.

The first time he beat me up mother was out and father was away. He beat me up and threw me over a wall. There were some neighbours around, young girls. I cried and then I said, 'I can feel blood on my face. I'll show mother that you hurt me. It's bleeding, my face is, and my arm.' 'Bleeding?' he said, 'let me see. Show me the blood.' I showed him my wet arm. 'This is it, there's blood there.' He laughed. 'Blood. That's not blood, that's saliva. Stupid, she thinks that's blood. Blood is red, stupid.' Until then I had not realized that blood was red. I thought the wet sticky patch on my arm was blood. I was blind, could not see the colour, did not know that blood was red. I felt belittled and ignorant. I could not see. Bitter. The bitterness I felt. He used to hit me on the head and pull my hair. Handfuls of my hair would come away.

When we lived in the village my father would take Ali with him on his journeys. It was common that the first son was taken by the father from an early age to learn a trade, to prepare him for the future, for manhood. He was sent to a school, which the mullahs ran in the village, once or twice a week and later on every morning. But later still he stopped going. We had to pay the mullahs with some bread or crops every so often, and often could not afford it. I was happy when he went off with father and we did not have to have him around.

Some time after we had moved to Teheran, he was apprenticed to a tailor. He began by doing the cleaning in the tailor's shop and then gradually learned the skills of his trade. Now as an apprentice, he had to travel a long way to get to the shop. He spent maybe two or three hours walking every day. We couldn't afford the bus fare. I think the hardship in his life hardened him further, whereas Akbar did not harden at all. He was caring and giving. Ali used to try to convince Akbar he should become a chauffeur. 'A chauffeur? Do you want me to be a chauffeur in the house of a military man or a crook businessman and open and close the car door for his wife?' Akbar would say. 'No, thank you. I'll be what I want to be. I want to be a lorry driver and I want to be my own boss.' As he grew older Akbar had many of my father's characteristics: giving, adventurous, good-hearted, willing to take risks.

On one occasion father had a fight with the man in the shop above our basement room. The shopkeeper spoke Farsi, and thus regarded himself as smarter than father. I remember father's fury, frustration and helplessness. But the man had the upper hand.

Father became weak, depressed and unhappy. We had to move away from that basement. We took a little room in a house nearby. There were three, four other households in that house as well. Each family had a room. There were four or five members in each family, like us. We were five. In that house, in the yard, there were pine trees which gave shade where I used to play on hot summer days. We had a tiny room. It was there that mother and father's relationship went very bad. They used to quarrel often.

We used to cry when they quarrelled. Father used to threaten mother. Mother used to say, 'If you dare, you just dare to lift a hand to me. If you just dare then you're no man.' She wouldn't speak to him for days.

Father found it hard to accept that his wife earned more than he did. 'I don't need you really, do I?' mother would say, 'I can bring up my children all on my own.' She felt stronger, living nearer her own relatives and managing to work and to feed her own family. She felt in control. She had power. Father, the opposite. He felt disarmed, his power taken away, his role as breadwinner lost, less of a man, less of a husband. 'You are even more useless than a woman,' mother would say to him, 'look how I manage and look at you. What do you do?' Those words burned father's heart.

My mother was not a man-hater. She hated my father, and her first husband because she'd been forced into marriage with them. She had not made her own choice. She hated sex, hated my father for it. I witnessed one of those sex sessions, in that basement room of ours. We were all sleeping round the *korsi*. I slept in the corner next to them. In the middle of the night I was woken up by father pleading with mother. Mother was furious. She was refusing him. He was pleading. 'Please, only this once, only this time.' 'Leave me alone, I said,' mother said with fury. 'For God's sake, leave me alone. Damn on you. May your father rot in hell.' Mother gave in. The act started. 'May your father rot in hell,' mother sounded like thunder. An extraordinary feeling took over me. I felt intense pressure in my pelvis, a terrible disturbance and restlessness. I called father. 'I want to go to the toilet,' I kept saying. They were quiet for a moment. I kept repeating it. If any of us needed to go to the toilet in the middle of the night, it was father's responsibility to take us out into the street, where there was a lavatory. 'Shut up, you,' father said, but he took me outside. I could feel the intense discomfort in his voice. He was impatient and cross. When I got there I could not wee. I tried to force it.

Father was standing just outside, listening. Nothing. I had disturbed father for nothing.

Mother decided to leave my father. Mother was packing her things and father was crying. I could tell from his voice he was crying, his voice was shaking, breaking. My mother's brother, my uncle, came over. 'Please, please, don't take her away,' my father begged him. 'Don't break my home.' Uncle didn't say anything. Mother packed everything we needed — clothing mostly — and then took us with her and we left. We left father.

Father fell ill soon afterwards. Once I visited him with mother. He was in bed. He was very weak, his voice could just about be heard. Mother fed him. He said he didn't want anything. He hadn't eaten for days. That was the last time I saw him alive.

The night before the visit I'd had a dream. I dreamt that we were to go to visit him and someone told me that I should not go, if I did father would die. The next day, when we did go, I told him this. 'Father, I had a dream last night. Someone told me I shouldn't come to see you because you would die.' There was silence for a minute and then I heard him speak. His voice was shaky, whispery. 'And yet, you did come.' He was very upset. 'One wouldn't visit one's enemy with this dream.' Those were his last words to me. That was the last time I heard his voice.

The next thing I knew was that father was to be brought over to us. We lived in my uncle's house, in a room at the back of his grocery shop. We had to get father to the doctor. It was a summer's day and they laid father in the shade, in front of our room. The atmosphere was one of understanding that he was dying, but that he should still be taken to the doctor. A cousin of mother's, a young man, lifted him to carry him to the doctor's at the top of the street. 'No, no, put him down,' someone cried. Father had wet himself. It was then they touched him. He was cold. 'He's gone,' they said. I started laughing. I couldn't stop laughing. Mother and the other women started to cry. Mother smacked me and someone sat me down next to father, next to his body. I started crying.

After father's death, mother went through a very disturbing time. She was mourning. She cried often.

Ali said, 'We should put Monir in the orphanage.' Mother repeated it in front of me. 'Ali says that we should put Monir in the orphanage.' I felt mother agreed with this and only social pressure stopped her doing so.

We all got birth certificates. The official was taking down the details, and he came to me and asked, 'How old is she?' Mother paused for a moment, then replied, 'Oh, she's only ten.' Mother did not expect me to marry but she kept to the tradition and gave my age as older than it was. What had prompted her to say that? Whatever the reason, I was registered about four years beyond my actual age. My older brother Ali had been registered at birth, but myself and Akbar, my younger brother had not. It was thanks to that kind man, the manager of the garage where father had worked, that we were registered. Having a birth certificate would help us receive occasional benefits and grants, he suggested.

The other man at the garage, the shopkeeper who had despised father, proposed to mother. Mother wanted very much to marry him but she said no, probably because of what others might say. At times I wondered if anything went on between them. Mother definitely felt for him.

CHAPTER EIGHT

We lived in a little room at one end of my uncle's house. Our room was about ten feet square. From it a little window led into the grocery shop run by the younger of my uncles, and underneath was a cellar and the lavatory. The main house was at the other end of the garden, with a big pond in the middle. Every week I used to help grandmother empty and clean the pond and change the water. Uncle liked flowers. They had cottonwool plants and lots of geraniums and flowers growing all around the pond. Each evening I would help grandmother water the flowers. The garden was about three hundred metres long. The main house had four rooms, two downstairs and two upstairs. My uncle Ahmad and his wife lived upstairs, as well as the younger uncle who ran the grocery shop, my grandmother, and Aziz, the son of a great uncle of mother's. Uncle looked after Aziz. The two downstairs rooms were rented, one to each family. There must have been around eighteen or twenty people living in that house of five rooms and a shop. Many others visited and stayed for a few days — relatives of mother's and uncles and friends from their village.

Mother had three brothers. The oldest, Habib, still lived in the village in Khorbendeh and had the family property. And a divorced sister who also lived in the village, used to visit occasionally. And there was Uncle Ahmad who looked after his younger brother, the uncle who now ran the grocery. Uncle Ahmad was eight years old when he started working in the café. Eventually he held a partnership there. Because of his success he was able to feed all the relatives and send their children to school. He was like a father to everyone in the family. There was a place in his heart for everyone. If anyone died or was in hardship in the family, Uncle Ahmad was the protector, the consultant, who shared people's troubles and gave them advice on how to cope, how to deal with crises and hardship. He helped people get back on their feet again. He was largely self-taught but valued education, and paid for the children to be educated, including my brother Akbar. We didn't see much of him. He used to come home late in the evenings and some nights he didn't come home at all. He stayed in the café apparently. The café was a long way away — maybe two or three hours of travel, horse-drawn carriage then by bus. In the mornings he used to get up late. He had breakfast in the garden by the pond in the summer. He liked fruit for breakfast. During breakfast he used to get Akbar and Aziz to read their homework and he would correct it and share any left over fruit with us. He hardly spoke to me. I existed but just in the background for him. I didn't feel he resented me, or avoided me. He didn't take any particular interest in me. There was nothing to take interest in. Once, when I was standing on the landing I bent down and looked out of the open window. He saw me and said, 'She's bending down,' and they told me off, to move from the window. What didn't he like? Was it because my hair was not covered? Was he worried that I might fall? For some time I wondered why he did not want me to bend down at that window. That was the only time he took any notice of me.

After some time mother became very unhappy in that house. She started to fight with my uncle's wife Goli. She was a lively young girl, energetic, enthusiastic and good-hearted. Mother resented her and was jealous of her. Mother said Goli did not deserve Uncle Ahmad, she just was not good enough. Mother hit herself on the head whenever she became enraged and pulled at her hair, just as she had whenever she quarrelled with father. Sometimes she used to faint, and then someone would bring smelling salts to place under her nose to bring her round. On one occasion she took an overdose of opium. She was taken to hospital and her stomach was pumped. After that she decided to move. She wanted to be independent, and to run her own life, our lives, to be in control. In that household she really didn't have much of a place. She was respected. She was consulted over the cooking and sewing and the making of the preservatives, the pickling and drying of food for winter, but somehow she wasn't satisfied. She wanted something more, to determine how she herself lived, to be free of that system, to get out into the world and meet new people, take on challenges, be successful. So she found work in the area we'd lived before. Eventually she took a room there, and we all moved into the one room, in a house with two other families.

Mother worked for the family who lived upstairs. The woman was called Hamideh Khamnom. She was a small, petite and kind woman. She spoke Turkish and was, in fact, an acquaintance of my father's former garage manager. Her husband worked in a factory making metal beds. They had two rooms upstairs, one large and one small. Mother used to do their washing, their cleaning, and looked after their children. Occasionally she went out to do the washing for other families as well.

Mother became happier, more contented and she seemed to find her feet again. She was positive, optimistic and very active, full of energy. She would not stop for a minute. She was young, and would go from house to house and she made a number of friends. She could pick and choose now, and would keep the clients she liked. If she did not like a family, she would not go back there again. She was happy, the happiest I had ever known her. Those days I think were the happiest days in her life ever — in charge, in control, successful, at the height of her creativity. She was quite a talented woman. She only had to look at somebody's dress and she would come home straight away and copy it from memory. It would come out beautifully. She used to cut out and sew chadors and dresses for people, and do patchwork and embroidery. She was an excellent cook. She would pick up ideas for all kinds of recipes from the houses where she worked and she would come home and experiment. Some of the women she worked for became her friends. They liked her. She was likeable, positive, she had a positive effect on people though she understood her position all the time.

Her relatives did not speak to her for some time because she had left them, walked out without any discussion first, moved us all out. Uncle Ahmad especially was worried, but gradually, as they saw that she was making a success of her life and how much happier she was, they came round. We all got together again on New Year's Day, the first away from them, and that was wonderful. My mother was so happy to see them again. She felt complete, having re-established her connection with them and they respected her more.

The man who owned the house we lived in was divorced. He had a small boy. The story went round that his wife had divorced him because of his impotence. Mother wasn't interested in him. She set a limit on his visits. Those days were certainly my mother's best days ever and our best days as a family together. I helped mother around the house and helped look after the children upstairs as well. Even I was happy there, the happiest I had been. Mother started buying new things, bit by bit, for the house — a little saucepan one day, a frying pan the next, or a new kettle or samovar, and each time she bought something new she felt wonderful. We all felt happy, satisfied, enjoyed it, for each item gave us enjoyment and pleasure for months.

CHAPTER NINE

The owner of the house, disappointed by mother's rejection, wanted us out. He told us he was going to sell the house, so we had to move. Mother had to find another room for us. She walked along the streets, knocking on each door as was the custom. 'Have you got empty rooms?' 'Yes, how many of you?' 'I've got three children. And I work, I'm a washerwoman.' 'No, not with three children. And a washerwoman.' They weren't prepared to give us room. This was before they even knew that she had a blind girl. It worried her — how was she going to break the news of her blind daughter if she were to find a room? Should she keep it quiet until we moved in? She did not share this worry or show it, but I felt it. It was hard finding a room. It went on and on for months and months, mother looking, worrying. In the end she found one. A woman named Fatemah Khanom was prepared to take us in. Her husband was away working in construction, building houses — she had three children herself. We moved in. She was Turkish and we got on well.

I don't quite know how mother told her the news that I couldn't see. They didn't seem to mind. The day her husband returned home, mother was away working. I felt I shouldn't show myself. I closed the door and stayed in the room listening to everything that went on in the house. What if he sees me and knows that I can't see? If he finds out I'm blind what would he do? Would he ask us to leave and then where would we go? Could he throw us out if he discovers I'm blind? I stayed in for hours, did not leave the room. The lavatory was outside at the other end of the garden as usual. Let me see, how could I reach it without his noticing that I can't see? I'll have to walk without revealing that I was unsure of myself. I imagined the path and each step I had to take, and exactly where things stuck out. What if I had to fetch water? Well, I'd have to do without. I'd wash myself next time. And then nothing happened, nothing was said. He didn't seem to have any objections to my blindness.

The house was the first on the right in a narrow alleyway, off a slightly wider alleyway, neither wide enough for a car to drive through. It was behind a main road, in Sarsabil, south Teheran. We had the downstairs front room. Other tenants lived in the back room, and Fatemah Khanom lived upstairs with her three children. Normally the front room was smaller, with a small window on to the street, and cheaper, which was why we took it. The back room would usually be the nicest room in the house, large, with a big window to the garden, south facing, with plenty of sunshine, but we never could afford that. We never managed to occupy a back room. That was a dream for us.

Fatemah was kind and considerate, especially towards me. She seemed to understand my predicament. Now and then she gave me something good — whatever she cooked — a little bit more to me. I could have a taste of anything. She liked giving me treats, as though she understood how much I suffered, how little I had, how unwanted I was. She tried to give me nourishment to enable me to carry on. 'Monir, come upstairs, come and play with the children,' she would say, sensing my despair. She knew I loved going upstairs to her rooms and playing with her children, and occasionally maybe getting little treats. Just being up there was a treat for me, being away from my family where I was not wanted. I used to be there, up there, for hours and then mother would call me. 'Come down, you are being a nuisance.' 'Leave her,' Fatemah would say, 'she's no bother, honestly.' Fatemah used to be my refuge when my brother beat me up. I used to run up there and hide from him, and would be comforted by her. Once I ran upstairs and he followed me and beat me in front of Fatemah and the children, pulled my hair out, banged my head against the wall. I found the hair afterwards on the floor. They'd tried to stop him. He beat me even harder. I was bruised all over. I slept upstairs that night with them. The next day was Friday, a holiday, and they took me to the zoo. I was very unhappy, I did not enjoy the outing. They tried to buy me treats and make me happy but I could not cheer up. I was deeply miserable, unhappy. I became acutely aware of the fact that I had to get out of there. I had to find some way of leaving that place, of freeing myself from that anguish. Anywhere would be better than there, better than home.

My brother's resentment had increased. 'She's just an extra mouth to feed,' he would say. 'What's the use of having her around?' Then I started thinking of getting myself out from there. I had to do something. I didn't know what, but I had to do something. I was restless. I had to escape from there, and from my brother. He was growing older, stronger, more aggressive, demanding, self-important. He went to work. He earned money. Only a few pounds a week, but he was bringing something home. Mother started losing her control of him, he was beating up my younger brother savagely. Mother was becoming frightened of him too. She could not stop him when he was in a rage. He was getting the upper hand, all the time, and this worried me a lot. This I could not go on living with. I had to do something for myself. Even when he was not there, that room seemed to me like a torture chamber.

When the families my mother worked for went away on holiday, they sometimes left her the key so that she could go and water the flowers and check the house. I loved going with her, everything just felt so lovely in those houses, it was the freedom I loved most.

We got friendly with our neighbours. Our neighbour on the left had a telephone. I used to go there often. They liked me and they let me use their telephone at times. 'Come to us any time you like,' they would say, 'stay here as long as you like.' They had a large garden with lots of flower beds round the pond, and a hallway with cool tiles that I walked on in bare feet on hot summer days. I used to like lying down on the tiles in the coolness. A young woman lived next door with her husband on the right. She had no children. I made friends with her. I used to go to her house. I loved visiting neighbours, getting away from our cramped, dark room where my brother's power reigned. In other people's houses, I was treated with respect. It was wonderful. Somehow I was aware that I must not abuse the neighbours' hospitality. I always waited until I was invited, although I longed to be able to visit more often. They were my life support, those neighbours. I became friends with the daughter of the family in the house opposite us. She was a bit older than me. She went to school. I often sat in the alleyway with her or went to her house. She hardly came to my place, I did not invite her much, I did not dare to invite anyone to the house. It had this horrible atmosphere of fear, cruelty, punishment, it wasn't a place for joy, pleasure, play, visits. Besides I had to remember that we were tenants. We always had to be careful not to make too much noise, not to slam the door, not to create bother in case the landlady might be upset. But in the neighbours' houses I felt so free. Their houses were spacious. There I felt light, comfortable, happy, a different person.

The schoolgirl, my friend, read out her homework to me, and we learned together. Sometimes we would sit in the alleyway. She would bring out her books and read from them, and I would in turn explain to her what she had read. 'How do you know all this, Monir? You don't go to school.'

'No, but I understand.'

'But how?' she would ask in surprise. 'How do you understand? I don't and I go to school. And you don't and yet you understand. Tell me how.'

'Well, I listen to the radio. I listen to everyone who talks and I try to learn from everyone.'

'Yes, but my school's not on radio. How do you understand?'

'I don't know how. I wish I could go to school. I would learn there.'

'You don't need to go to school, really,' she would laugh. 'You understand everything.'

Her mother sometimes invited us in. 'Come girls, come inside, it's too noisy there for you to study.' I was pleased to be included with her 'girls' — that was me as well. She included me, 'girls'. I would go in eagerly. And we would go to a quiet corner to study. The trouble was we did not like sitting indoors because it was hot, but outdoors it was noisy everywhere. Sometimes we had difficulty finding a quiet corner in the garden to study. We used to talk about all sorts of things. Having periods, having babies and so on. 'I don't want to marry. I want to be a teacher or a nurse,' she would say. What about me, I wondered, what am I going to be? I would keep quiet when she talked about her future. 'What are you going to be?' she would ask me.

'I don't know. I know I sweep the room and wash the dishes and sometimes cook when my mother's gone to work but I feel I'm not doing anything. I wish I could go to school like you do. But I know it's not possible.'

'How about you coming to the class with me?' she would say. And I would laugh, 'That would be funny wouldn't it? I wouldn't understand a word.'

'Why don't I talk to my teacher and ask her if you could come with me one day to school, see what it's like? I'll tell her that you help me with my homework. You know she knows about you.'

'Oh, no. No. Never, never tell her about me. That's impossible. Me coming to your class.' I felt ignorant. It would be a waste of time and everyone would laugh at me, I said to myself. As the days went by I grew more and more unhappy. My younger brother's screams would petrify me. There was a sense of terror in the atmosphere and I desperately wanted to run away from it, I did not know how, where. I considered suicide. I had tried once before.

A few years earlier — I must have been about five or six — we were living in Fezahanung's house near uncle's house. The owner of the house used to smoke opium. There was always a *maghal*, firetray, in the hall. She would sit there on a little mat and some cushions and smoke away. I could smell it when she smoked. I knew she kept the opium somewhere under the mangle. One day when nobody was home I went and looked for it. I found it in a little box. There were lumps of sticky opium. I took one and brought it home. I said goodbye to all the things I liked in the room. Nobody was in the house. It was all right. I could do it now. I cut off a bit and swallowed it with water and put the rest in a little bag made out of cloth and hung it around my neck. That was how secrets were carried. If mother had any money or anything precious she would hang it around her neck and would keep it under her clothes. And then I kissed the things I liked and lay down on the floor, put a chador over me. I was sure I would not wake up. I fell asleep but after a while I did wake up. I was fine. I was surprised. I thought opium would kill me if I took a big enough dose. Obviously I had not taken enough. The thought of suicide was comforting. I had something to fall back on. I thought of how I felt before I took the opium, as I lay down with the chador over me. I would die in sleep. It was soothing, comforting. I carried the rest of the opium with me round my neck for a while. I threw it away in the end.

CHAPTER TEN

I often listened to the radio. In fact, the radio was my only real source of information. I always listened to the news. My brother was annoyed. 'How do you understand the news? What do you think you understand?' 'I like listening to the news,' I said. One day when I was in despair, wondering who I could go to, who I could turn to, I thought, If only I could talk to someone on the telephone. I decided to go next door where there was a telephone. The family had told me that I could go to their house and use the phone if I wanted. I had their key. I let myself in. The house was empty. I phoned a radio programme, *Home and Family* which went out every morning. It was a problem hour — people would write in with their problems and these would then be discussed and a solution or suggestion offered. I rang up. I couldn't stop crying. I asked to talk to the people on that programme. A man answered, 'You can talk to me. What is the problem?' he asked in a gentle sympathetic voice. I could not talk. I kept crying. I cried for a long time but he just listened. 'I'm sorry,' I managed to get out finally. 'Don't worry, I'm here. I'll listen to you as long as you need me to,' he said. I couldn't believe it. That made me cry more. Somebody wants to listen to me. I don't know how long this went on, eventually I managed to talk. I explained my situation, that my family didn't want me really, that my brother beat me up, very badly sometimes. 'I visit upstairs. I have neighbours but I can't talk to them about these problems. I don't know what to do. I'm sure my brother will do away with me somehow. He'll get rid of me. He has said that they should put me in an orphanage. Mother said it in front of me. The only reason I'm still here is that people would talk if they did put me in an orphanage. I just want to get away. I want to get out of this place. Please help me. Do you know anywhere, anything at all?'

'Listen, tell me, where you live. We'll come and visit you. I'll come with a lady,' he said, 'a colleague of mine.' 'I can't. I can't tell you where I live. I don't know what they will think. My family, my mother, they would be upset. What would they do to me if I did?'

'Well, listen, let me suggest something else. Why don't you write us a letter? Get someone to help you to write all the things you have told me and then we'll talk about it on the radio. I'm sure something will come out of it. I assure you something will.'

'Oh, that's a good idea. I think I will.'

'Have you got anyone to help you write the letter?'

'Yes. My next door neighbour. But I can't tell her all these things I have told you.'

'No, you don't have to. Just tell her whatever you can. I'll remember your name. And I'll make sure you get some help. Trust me. I will do that for you, and take care. I'm sorry you're unhappy.'

'Goodbye,' I said and I sobbed and sobbed. It was a big house and I did not have to worry that anyone would hear me. I don't know how many hours I cried in that house. My throat was bursting. My eyes dried up. My head was splitting. But I felt better. I'd been listened to. The man on the radio had been on the phone to me. He did not think that I was wasting his time. He didn't tell me off. He listened to me. He understood me, offered a suggestion. It was a good idea. I would write and he said he would remember me.

The thought of the letter grew stronger in me every day, I kept thinking about how to word it, how much to write, what to say. I worked on it all in my head. Every day, every night, I would to go sleep with it and I would wake up with it. I used to have dreams about it, how I should write the letter. I visited Aghdas Khanom who lived next door. She was in her early twenties, a kind, gentle, and sensitive girl. I always enjoyed going to her house. She was lonely. She had no children. She was educated, she could read

and write, she was the best person to ask. She was on my side I felt. I asked her, 'Will you write a letter for me?'

'Yes. Who to?'

I explained everything.

'Yes, of course I will. You tell me what you want to write and I'll write it.' She wrote down everything I said and then she read it back to me and asked me if I wanted any charges. 'No, it was fine.' So we posted it.

I did not tell anybody. I listened to the problem hour every day. After about a week my letter came up. A man and a woman ran the programme. One of them announced: 'We have a letter from a young girl. It goes like this. "Dear Sir, I'm writing to you because I am desperate, I hope you will be able to help me. I am thirteen and I am blind. I live with my mother and two brothers in a room. My mother goes out to work every day. She's a washerwoman. My older brother works in a tailor's shop and my younger brother goes to school. He's in Grade Four. I stay home all day. I have nothing to do. I get bored. This makes me feel depressed, unhappy. There is nothing for me to do. I am not using my mind, I feel I am not doing anything useful. I help mother at home by doing housework but this is not enough for me. I help my younger brother with his schoolwork. He reads out his homework and I help him to understand it. After he has read it out to me I understand and then I explain it to him, his maths and everything. I have a friend who goes to school. She reads out her books to me and I understand them as well. And I explain them to her. I learn from them and then I teach them, both my friend and my brother. But this is not enough, I feel I would like to learn a lot more. You see I feel that if I can learn now then when I grow up I can teach. There must be somewhere where I can learn, I need help to find it. Will you help me? Please. I don't want to spend all my life sitting at home and doing nothing. This is torture. I am unhappy. Everyone else goes to school and they understand. There must be something for me to do somewhere. I listen to the radio a lot and I learn a lot from radio. I need to find somewhere to learn. I need to learn desperately. Please help me. Yours sincerely, You are my only hope.'"

The man's voice was familiar. He was the one I'd talked to on the phone. They spent quite a bit of time on my letter. They discussed my problem and kept saying that they hoped any listener with any ideas would ring them up. 'There must be something, it's just a matter of finding it,' they said. 'She's an intelligent girl,' the man said, 'she deserves help. I hope we'll be able to do something for her. We will wait for our listeners' suggestions. We will write to you, Monir, don't give up hope.'

I was excited. I had found friends, some people on my side. I had faith in them. A couple of days later a letter came. I took the letter to Aghdas Khanom straight away, and she opened it with excitement and read it to me. 'Dear Monir, Since we broadcast your letter a listener has contacted us, somebody called Dr Vahidi. Dr Vahidi is willing to help you; here is her telephone number. If you ring her, she will make an appointment for you to go and see her. She knows of a school for the blind in Isfahan where you can go. Good luck and keep in touch. If you have any problem, get back to us.'

At last there was light at the end of the tunnel. Aghdas Khanom shared my sense of hope. We told mother, and Aghdas Khanom read the letter to mother. She couldn't believe it. 'God is good,' mother kept muttering to herself, 'my prayers have been answered.' I had heard her ask in her prayers for some opening for me. Some opening — we did not know what. She asked for it. I asked for it all the time. We looked for it and now it seemed it might be there. I had to phone. I rushed to our next door neighbour, to ask if I could use the phone. 'Of course you can,' she said. I dialled the number. A woman answered. I asked for Dr Vahidi. 'She's not here at the moment. Ring her in the evening when she'll be home from work,' the voice said. 'I'll ring in the evening,' I replied excitedly, hopefully. The phone call had been genuine, the number was the right one, it had not been a hoax. I could not wait.

In the evening I rushed to the phone. The same voice answered. 'She's seeing patients at the moment. Ring in about half an hour's time, she'll be free then to talk to you.' I rang again. The same voice answered. 'Yes. It's Monir.' The doctor came to the phone. I could hardly believe my own ears. She existed. She was interested in me. She wanted to help me. 'Come and see me tomorrow evening with your mother. I'll give you my address, can you remember?' She told me the address and explained to me how to get there. 'I'll be there tomorrow afternoon.'

I was excited, anxious. Mother was anxious too, I felt. The news went round. Everyone knew, all the family and the neighbours, relatives and friends, everyone knew what was happening, what I had done. 'Monir's written this letter to the radio and a doctor, a lady doctor, is offering to help.' I suddenly became important. My brother was surprised. How did I think of it? people asked. I could not explain. No one could guess my motives, the intensity of my despair and desire to escape from that house.

CHAPTER ELEVEN

Early afternoon the next day we set off. With me were mother and another woman, a neighbour. We had to catch two buses. We allowed plenty of time to reach Dr Vahidi's apartment because she lived in the centre of town. After a couple of hours we arrived and walked up the stairs, to the third floor, and rang the bell. A woman let us in. We had to sit and wait, while Dr Vahidi saw the patients. This was her clinic as well as her home. It was a big apartment with five or six rooms, and a large hall used as a waiting room. People were coming and going. This was her private clinic and she was a gynaecologist. We sat and waited.

After a while, when the clinic was finished, she came out. She came straight towards me. 'Hello, Monir,' she said and put her hand on my shoulder. I tried to stand up as a sign of respect. 'Sit down,' she pushed on my shoulder with her hand. For a moment she was silent. She seemed to be wondering which of the two women was my mother. 'I am her mother,' mother explained.

'What is your name?'

'Mahi,' mother replied. 'Mahi, how long has Monir been blind?' Mother told her the history of my blindness.

'Has she had any treatment?' Mother told her how I had had one operation, a corneal graft performed by Professor Sharam at the state hospital, soon after we settled in Teheran. Nothing had come of it. For me it was almost as if it had not happened.

I must have been six or seven. I had no idea what was happening but I did not believe that I could regain my sight. I remember how the patients had shouted for bedpans and nobody responded, and how I went to get the bedpans and then emptied them. I found shoe heels or bits of rubber in the food, all kinds of rubbish in the stews. I remembered a patient who had been discharged shouting he had nowhere to go. He would not leave and Professor Sharam had pushed him down the stairs swearing at him. I heard the nurses saying, 'Poor man, what will happen to him now, he's out on the streets?'

Dr Vahidi listened to mother patiently with her hand still on my shoulder. She said she wanted to look at my eyes and took me out to the light. 'I'd like to take you to an eye doctor first, an eye specialist.' 'Professor Sharam?' I said quickly.

'No, not him. He's an old man now. I don't think he knows what he's doing,' she laughed. 'No, this doctor is called Dr Mehdi. He's a friend of mine. I'll see what he thinks about your eyes. He might be able to do something for you,' and she told us she knew of a school. 'It's a school for the blind in Isfahan. It's for girls. Run by English missionaries. The woman in charge is wonderful. All the girls call her Mama. You'll be very happy there, you will learn a lot. I can arrange that for you if you want me to.'

'Oh, yes please,' I said. 'You are very kind,' mother said gratefully.

'Would you like to stay with me here tonight?'

I kept silent. I didn't know what to say. This was too much too soon, too quick. Dr Vahidi turned to my mother. 'Would you like to leave her here tonight with me? She can stay with me as long as she likes and I'll arrange everything. She's an intelligent girl, your daughter. I like her. I'd like to help her.'

'You are very kind, Dr Vahidi. May God reward you, no one else can help us.'

She asked me again. 'Do you feel like staying here with me, Monir?'

'Yes, I would, please,' I said, with excitement I could hardly control. 'You can come and visit her tomorrow if you like, or ring. Monir can stay with me as long as she likes.'

Mother and her friend said goodbye and left me there.

I found my way about her apartment. Opposite her bedroom was the bathroom. A door opened from her bedroom into her consulting room and another door led to the hall. There was a sitting room, a dining room and a day room where I was to sleep. The waiting room with seats all round it, and the kitchen.

Dr Vahidi and I became friends quickly. She showed me how to use the kitchen. I started to make tea for the patients, to open the door for them and show them to the waiting room. I answered the telephone and relayed messages. Gradually I took over from her helper. I became the secretary/receptionist and housekeeper. Her part-time helper left and I took her place. It was fun. There was no time to listen to the radio now. I talked to people in the clinic. I talked on the telephone. I loved learning, and learning to speak in a more educated way.

Mother occasionally came to visit and then she started coming once a week, to do the cleaning. She didn't get paid but she liked doing it because of me. I was happy.

Some weeks later Dr Vahidi arranged my visit to see Dr Mehdi, the eye specialist. We went to his private clinic. Dr Mehdi said there was a chance. He would do a corneal graft. 'It is the cornea that is damaged. I think the nerve is all right. She'll have some sight, so that's hopeful.' It would take about a month to get a bed in the private hospital and Dr Vahidi agreed to pay all the fees for an operation on my left eye.

I did not hope or believe that I could regain sight. It was not possible. Just as I had no hope that the first operation would be successful. Dr Vahidi, however, seemed excited. Maybe I was protecting myself against disappointment. I just went along with it without any expectation. Getting away from home, from my brother, having a new life, this was enough for me. It wasn't sight I was searching for. I sometimes overheard Dr Vahidi talk about me. 'She's terrific. She's an intelligent girl. Very clever indeed. She irons for me beautifully, makes tea, looks after all my patients, takes messages. She's got an excellent memory. I wish I could learn from her, she amazes me, she's so quick. She's such a capable girl.' I was happy that she was happy with me but I did not, could not, believe any of these things she was saying. I was not worthy of any of those kind words. I was pleased she trusted me, let me do her ironing, let me touch her things, handle delicate, expensive things of hers, clean them, touch them. 'I'm hoping to get her sight restored. She should have a good future,' she would say.

During the day Dr Vahidi worked at the hospital and in the evenings she had her private clinic and I looked after the patients. Some did not notice that I could not see. I moved about confidently, comfortably, so sure of myself. I was determined to succeed in my new job, new life, new image.

The day I went to hospital I wondered what her reaction would be if the operation failed. Would she withdraw all her attention? Would she send me home to live with my brother for ever? Is that where I'm doomed for life?

I was put in a room with two other patients. The nurses chatted and joked and laughed with me. I always laughed. Sometimes Dr Vahidi came and visited me. Mother came to see me. The corneal graft failed. I did not stop smiling. I did not show disappointment. 'All that money — for nothing,' I heard Dr Vahidi say. 'And that is only the hospital fee.' She did not pay the surgeon's fees from what I gathered. I worried that all that money had been wasted on me, all that effort, all that caring, the nurses, was I worth it? And Dr Vahidi was from Isfahan. Isfahanis, it was said, were tight fisted and mean.

After ten days I returned to Dr Vahidi's although the operation had failed, and her money had been wasted. I was embarrassed when I heard her say how disappointed she was. I wished the earth would open and swallow me. She said I could stay with her as long as I liked then she would arrange for me to go to the Blind School in Isfahan.

Time went by and she forgot about the Blind School. That did not worry me. I was happy as things were. I heard rumours that she was getting married, there was a man visiting her every day. She was going to marry him and move to his place north of Teheran, where the rich lived. She wanted me to go with her to her new home. She forgot all about my schooling, the great change in her life took over. I did not remind her. I had to be careful about asking for things, in case it upset her. Her husband-to-be was a rich businessman, with a large house, a big garden and a swimming pool.

Dr Vahidi had always brought back loads of drugs with her from the hospital and stored them under her bed. The pile would build up until the space under her bed was completely filled. Then a man, the chemist from downstairs, would come and take them all away. On one occasion, as he came out of her bedroom, he said to mother, 'I gave Dr Vahidi ten pounds to give you to pay you for your work.' Mother was excited and waited but Dr Vahidi never gave her the money. Mother reminded her what the man had said. 'To hell with him,' she said. She didn't hide anything. And later I learned from one of the nurses who used to come and spend her spare time working for Dr Vahidi that there had been an inquiry in the hospital about the missing drugs. It was a state hospital and much equipment and many drugs had gone missing and they were accusing some of the doctors of stealing them, so I put two and two together now I knew where the drugs came from. I thought of that money she withheld from mother.

Gradually Dr Vahidi sold her things and her apartment and moved to live with her husband. They were going on holiday and I was to stay with my family until they returned, when I was to ring them and go and stay with them. This I did. I went to see her in her new house, the large house with the big garden and the swimming pool. They had a cook, a chauffeur and a gardener and they entertained a lot. She had a ten-year-old nephew from Isfahan she was looking after. He went to school and we both slept in one room upstairs. It wasn't the same for me. There was not much for me to do, she did not have clinics any longer, I only answered the telephone, so I was idle again.

Her husband once made sexual advances to me, he cornered me and kissed me and kept saying, 'You kiss me as well, you've got to get married one day.' I didn't understand what was going on, I didn't like it, it took me by surprise. It was the first time in my life that a man had behaved like that to me. He was all shaky. I didn't know what was going on. Another time their cook touched my breast, so I told Dr Vahidi this in front of her husband and her husband got angry with the cook and gave him a slap. 'How dare you touch this girl,' he said angrily. 'Me touching this girl? Which girl?' the cook enquired with anger. 'This one here,' he said. I was standing next to Dr Vahidi. 'Is this a girl?' the cook said, 'Is this a girl?' he repeated. This incident stopped the husband's advances as well.

I was getting bored. I used the phone a lot. I used to pick it up and dial any number. If a young man answered, I started up a conversation. With one young man who worked in an office I formed a friendship. After a time I talked to him every day. He insisted on seeing me. 'Tell me where you live. I'd just love to see you, even from a distance. I promise I won't come near you if you don't want me. I'll just look at you, from a distance.' 'No,' I would make excuses. I did not want him to see me. I could not take the risk that he would find out that I was blind, that he would not talk to me again. One day I was sitting outside in the garden and the maid said, 'A young man is asking for you.' I knew who it was. Later I rang him. 'I saw you,' he said. 'I know your telephone number, I know where you live.' He was cross with me, I had disappointed him, did he think he was talking to a beautiful, rich, educated girl? Instead he saw me. I did not ring him again. 'What's wrong with our meeting?' he would ask. 'Nothing, it's just that my mother doesn't like me going out.' To myself I would say, 'There is something wrong, something seriously wrong.' My blindness, my looks. I have no education, I am not what you're used to. I am totally outside your experience. I was sad when I stopped talking to him. I felt like saying 'Please don't go away, please don't leave me, I love talking to you. I get so much pleasure from talking to you, hearing your voice, I learn from you.' I loved to learn, I searched for it desperately. The radio wasn't sufficient any longer.

Once mother and I were with Dr Vahidi in her chauffeur-driven car, and on the way she saw her cleaner walking. She was making for Dr Vahidi's home for a day's work. Dr Vahidi said 'hello' to her and then she said, 'I'll see you in the house,' and told the chauffeur to drive on. Then she said 'I did not want to give her a lift, otherwise she would expect too much from me.'

It was quite a long way to the house. It was a big car with plenty of room. The cleaner could easily have fitted in, I thought to myself. I remembered how my mother used to come home after walking long distances from work and collapse in exhaustion. Dr Vahidi's logic made no sense to me. As time went on I felt strongly that the situation wasn't right.

I had to do something. I was idle and my life was wasting away. Dr Vahidi seemed to have completely forgotten about the Blind School she suggested at the beginning. I went back to Aghdas Khanom and asked her to write a letter, this time to the Prime Minister's office. I explained that there was a school I'd heard of in Isfahan for the blind. 'I do want to go there. I do want to learn, please help me.' I received a letter back saying they had arranged for me to go to Isfahan, and they would pay my fees. I was to go there as soon as possible, taking the letter with me, everything had been arranged. This was wonderful, this was what I wanted. I was sad to leave my friends behind. Mother told uncle and he said he would accompany us to Isfahan.

CHAPTER TWELVE

On the coach trip to Isfahan, I felt sick and I slept most of the five or six hours of the journey, as I always did in times of intense anxiety. When we reached Isfahan we took a taxi straight to Noorain, the blind school, with the letter. They were expecting me. We entered a large hallway, cool, clean, lively. People were coming and going in every direction, dragging their feet, everyone talking. We were led to some seats on the right, under the stairs. The person in charge would see us shortly. In the meantime some of the girls came up and talked to us. 'Are you the new girl?' 'What is your name?' 'How old are you?' 'Where do you come from?' Question after question. Everybody was talking. They were laughing, they were all happy, one or two came up and touched me all over to see what I was wearing, my height, my shape. 'She's got long hair,' they called out to each other. 'Oh, it's beautiful.' This was strange for me. I was somewhat embarrassed. No one had touched me like this before; in fact I had not met any other blind person before.

'Hello, who is this?' one girl came up to me. 'Oh no, go away, leave her alone,' they all said with embarrassed laughter, trying to pull her away from me. 'Monir, she is funny, she will feel you all over and hug you and won't leave you alone, she's a bit, you know, funny in the head,' they all laughed. 'I want to see Monir,' she said in an innocent voice. 'Not yet, you'll see her later. Mama hasn't seen her yet. You wait your turn.'

'Mama?' I remembered. All the girls called the person in charge Mama. Mama arrived at this point, came straight over to me and shook hands with me. 'You are Monir? Welcome,' she said in Farsi. 'We're been expecting you.' She shook hands with my mother and uncle. 'You're her mother?' Yes,' mother replied shyly. They exchanged a few words. I was embarrassed at mother's strong accent. The girls whispered to each other, 'Oh, she's Turkish.' They giggled. I felt anxious, somewhat fearful, how were they going to treat me? They were all Farsi speakers. I didn't have a Turkish accent when I spoke Farsi but my mother's accent gave the game away.

'Come with me to the office,' Mama said. 'Mama' is halfway between 'mummy' and 'maman' (a Farsi word). We went to the office; mother gave her the letter from the Prime Minister's office. She looked at it. 'Yes, I know they have said they would pay for her. We are very pleased to have Monir here with us. She'll be very happy here.' 'Yes, we can see that everybody is very happy here,' said Uncle Ahmed. Mama had a very pleasant manner, I felt comfortable with her at once. Her voice was gentle, caring, competent, I felt comfortable, at ease. She had a happy voice, calm, down to earth, she spoke in broken Farsi. She apologized to my uncle and mother for speaking Farsi so badly. 'I have been here such a long time, I'm ashamed that I don't speak better Farsi,' she said. 'Monir can go home for holidays, is that all right?' She turned to me. It wasn't all right as far as I was concerned. I did not want to go back to that house ever again. I hoped they wouldn't send me by force, I said to myself. I kept quiet. My face must have reflected my thinking. 'You don't have to go if you don't want to,' she said kindly, 'but you can if you want to. I'm sure you would want to go after some time here, wouldn't you?' I kept quiet. She laughed, patting me on the shoulder, 'We'll see, all right? It's a long time till the holidays.' It was July and the next holiday was not until the following March.

'Are there any questions you would like to ask?' 'Can we come and see her?' uncle asked.

'Of course, any time. Any time you like.'

'We can write to her.'

'You can write to her as much as you like and she will write to you as well, I hope, won't you, Monir?'

I kept quiet.

'Come on, say something,' she laughed, patting me on the shoulder, 'won't you say anything?'

'Yes,' I replied, reluctantly.

'You can have a look around before you go, the girls will show you around. Are you staying the night in Isfahan?'

'Yes, we are,' said uncle. 'We'll come and say goodbye tomorrow.'

'That's fine.'

'Thank you for your kindness,' mother said in a sad voice. She was losing her daughter. She'd been wanting that for years and now it was actually happening. She felt sadness as well as relief. There was disbelief in her tone: 'was it really happening?' And a sense of failure. That she had not managed to look after me, to cope with me. And worry. 'Will she be all right?' They did not want to look round. They would do that tomorrow when they came to say goodbye properly. From the way she sounded mother must have looked very tired, very anxious. 'All the best, Monir. We'll come and see you tomorrow,' she managed to say, touching me. I stood motionless, did not respond. She kissed me, then they left.

The girls surrounded me, all waiting for me in the hallway, more and more of them coming and introducing themselves. 'She's from Teheran,' they kept telling each other. 'You are the second Teherani here, we have one Teherani already, we call her Shari, you'll meet her, she's in Teheran now on holiday with her family.' 'Come, we'll take you around and show you everywhere.' 'I want to take her arm.' 'Oh no, I was here first.' 'Oh please.' 'No.' 'I want to hold her arm now.' 'Later your turn.' 'All right then.' Two held on to my arms, one on each side, and two others held their arms, so five of us moved off in a row and the rest went ahead or behind. All chatting and talking about themselves, the school, about each other, and their friends away on holiday. 'There's a lot to show you. You see this is a big hallway. There are two staircases down, on either side of the front door. Now we'd better go upstairs first and show you your room. You're sharing a room with Zohreh. Where is Zohreh? Oh yeah, here you are, come on Zohreh. This is your room mate, the new girl. Her name is Monir.' And they went on talking about me, telling her my age and where I'd come from and so on. 'She's got long hair, two plaits, one each side, nice and thick and long, it's lovely.' 'Oh, let me touch it.' 'Oh no. Come on, later, you'll take my place,' Sakineh said laughingly. I was holding her arm by then. 'Zohreh is sixteen, Amra is thirteen.' They told me their ages and which grade they were in, how well they were doing and how well they spoke English. I heard them speak English. It was the first time I had heard a foreign language. 'Oh no, I can't learn this,' I didn't understand a word. 'How do you do it?'

They laughed. 'Oh well we just learn, you will learn.'

'Oh, I can't. Never.'

'Oh, you'll see, we'll teach you. You'll learn easily. We all had to learn it.'

I realized I had learnt one foreign language already — Farsi, and I could understand some Kurdish. The Turkish language, my father's tongue, I had mostly forgotten. It was a disgrace being Turkish, I thought. Since I had lived in Teheran where Farsi was the official language, and had stayed with Dr Vahidi who spoke excellent Farsi, I spoke with an educated accent. 'Hasn't she got a lovely accent. Teherani, she speaks beautifully.' As though they forgot I was a Turk. 'You sound quite educated, have you really not had any schooling? When did you lose your sight? You sound just like Shari, she's in Grade Eight and she's from Teheran. Her father's an engineer. They are well off. Do you have a father? What does he do?'

'Come along children.'

'What's happening?'

'Oh, Tahereh, come and meet the new girl, Monir.'

I was taken to my room. There was my bed. For the first time in my life I was going to sleep in a bed. I felt all around it. Then my wardrobe, a bedside cupboard. 'We'll bring your things up in a minute, and put them all away.' 'Do you want me to help you? I will if you want,' Zohreh said.

'Oh no, leave her alone, girls. I think she should do the unpacking herself. She doesn't want anybody to interfere and touch her things.'

'Oh, I'm her room mate after all,' Zohreh said. 'I can help you, can't I, Monir, if you want me to that is.'

'Oh Zohreh is just nosy, wants to know what you've got.' They laughed.

'No, honest to God no, I just want to help you.'

The room had a door leading to the balcony which ran along one side of the building. Each room opened on to the balcony as well as well as on to the corridor. In the summer the pupils slept out on the balcony. 'This is a new building' they told me. 'It only opened a couple of years ago. Princess Ashraf opened it — she's the Shah's twin sister. They've given a lot of money towards the building, in fact, they paid for the whole building. It cost, oh, hundreds of thousands of pounds. It's wonderful that they give so much money.' Later I found out that the school had substantial funding from the government and that it could have been totally government funded if they had been allowed control over staffing. This, the missionaries had not accepted. They wanted to choose their own staff — Christians.

I was shown over the whole building, all the rooms, and the bathrooms. There was a dispensary and the staff quarters where the staff had their own kitchen and dining room, their own maids and cook, and so on. Then there was a clothes room: 'There are lovely things in there, beautiful dresses, you'll get some, wait and see. They all come from abroad. They're all second-hand of course, but some beautiful things can be found in them. The Red Cross sends a lot, mostly from England.' It was a storeroom, mainly full of clothes.

The teenage pupils shared a double room. The children's room was a large dormitory with bunk beds sleeping about ten to fifteen children from five years down. Then there were two rooms for the boys from five to eight years old — after which they were sent to the boys' school run by German missionaries. The two schools worked closely together. Three girls in their early twenties, who were the stars, doing the highest grades, went outside to a sighted state school. They got everybody's special attention, and sometimes they were taken out to tea with sighted students.

Then there were the 'older girls' as they were called. There were five of them, with separate quarters downstairs. Each had a room to herself. They had their own dining room and their own washing room. They attended a craft workshop at the other end of the building weaving fabrics, and making tablecloths and so on which were sold. They made pretty things. 'Except for Mehir. She doesn't work,' they were explaining when I heard someone yelling, screaming and banging a door. 'Oh don't worry, Monir, that's only Mehir. She's dumb and deaf and blind and lame, that's all,' they laughed. 'She gets bored and can't talk so she just shouts. We don't go near her, she gets hold of us and feels us all over, all over our faces, and we don't like it. She's strange. Mama doesn't mind her feeling her. But she's clever, Monir. You know what? She threads a needle and does her own sewing. We can't do that. Sometimes we take a needle and thread to her and she threads it for us. Isn't that amazing?' They laughed. 'Nobody knows anything about her background. Nobody ever comes to see her. She must have been abandoned somewhere, we don't know where they found her. You'll hear her coming. Try to keep away from her. You can tell because she can't even walk properly, she just drags her feet. Something's wrong with one leg, it takes ages to get from A to B. She hangs on to things as she walks along, drags herself really. Sometimes when Mehir's shouting and screaming, Mama thinks she's calling somebody or she wants to tell us something. Mama goes and talks to her. Sometimes she goes to her room and sits with her, she thinks this makes her feel better. And in fact she is often quiet after that for a while. Maman says that she's very intelligent, but oh, we don't know about that,' they continued. She kept shouting and banging the door. Her voice was coming from the back of her throat, full and expressive. 'I think she must know Monir is here, she's asking to meet her,' said one of the girls.

'Oh yes, she's amazing. Although she can't hear, she senses things. I don't know how. She always knows if anything new or different is going on. She comes and wants to take part and keeps going until she finds out exactly what's happening,' said one of the others.

We walked downstairs, down one of the wide staircases which took us down to the older girls' quarters where the office was and also the study room, and the girls' sitting room. They showed me all the rooms except for the older girls' bedrooms. They took me to the dining rooms, one for the older girls, one for the children, one for us teenagers and those in their early twenties, and one for the servants as they were called. Then the kitchen, then the washrooms. We did our own washing up. They introduced me to the cook whose name was Hussein, 'but we all call him Uncle,' they said.

'He's a bit of a yokel and can be very rude, but take no notice.' He had a loud voice. I realized he would not stand for any nonsense, would not be messed about. The downstairs rooms opened outside on to a verandah underneath the balcony which went all round the house. There were many maids. Some worked in the washroom, washing everything by hand, some did general cleaning and some worked upstairs in the staff quarters. I was told no one was to bother them when they had their tea break or lunch break. I was surprised. A maid having a tea break! My mother never had a tea break. They were much better treated than I had ever seen, even in Dr Vahidi's house. The school was in a separate building, then I was shown the workshop and the showroom which sold the fabric, tablecloths, basket works and so on. There was also a swimming pool.

At about four o'clock the bell rang. 'It is tea time', the girls told me. 'You hear the bell for tea, for dinner, for lunch, for breakfast and for prayers. Oh yes, for prayers. You shouldn't be late. Very strict rule, you must never ever be late for prayers, and you must keep quiet during prayers, not talk, unless they say you can ask questions, or say a special prayer.'

'You will get to know everything quickly,' one of them said, sensing my confusion, bewilderment. 'Don't worry, we'll tell you everything, we'll show you everything.' We went down to the dining room for tea. The girls brought their own sugar from the cupboards in the wash room. 'You'll be given some soon.' They offered me some. 'Uncle will give you sugar and you'll have a cupboard to keep things in.' We each took a cup to the room where the tea was served and when it was poured out for us, we carried it to the dining room to drink. 'I want to sit next to Monir.' 'Oh no, I want to.' 'No, well I'm sitting here now.' We settled eventually, as many sitting at my table as it could take.

All this attention. I didn't know what to do with it. Was it really true? Was this me? So many people want to be close to me. The talk continued after tea. We talked and talked or rather I listened to them and sometimes I answered their questions. I was a good listener, they told me afterwards, many times. The bell went again, six o'clock, this was prayer time. We all had to assemble in the big hall. It was a very big hall with a stage at one end and it had eight doors which opened to the corridor and eight doors, which opened out on to the verandah. We all gathered for prayers at one end of the hall.

Prayers were twice daily: eight to nine in the morning and six to seven in the evenings. Everyone had to be there promptly, no one was to be late. We sang hymns, read from the Bible, discussed certain points from the Bible, and ended with prayers for everyone, particularly for the royal family — this prayer was quite detailed and quite long. It included all the authorities of Isfahan, the mayor, the governors, the police force, the army, the lot, asking the Lord's blessing for them and thanking them for their help and for the security they made for us. This was repeated with even more emphasis in the church every week. The church service lasted an hour in the morning and an hour in the evening and we had to go to one of them, whether we believed or not, we had to be sitting there in the church. Going to church was compulsory, we were told, unless someone were ill, the only excuse for not going.

Next day, mother and uncle came to say goodbye. They'd stayed in a hotel. Mother had stayed in a hotel for the first time in her life. She found it very strange. 'I couldn't lie down on the bed,' she said. 'I had to get on to the floor.' She hadn't slept at all with worry. 'I'm leaving my daughter here, maybe for ever, with foreigners, they are not even Muslims. What will become of her? What will become of me without her? What will people say? — that I've abandoned my daughter, left her so far away, with foreigners.' She was to say repeatedly, 'If you become a Christian, the milk I've given you will no longer be blessed.' They had a quick look round. Mother was quiet, hardly said anything. I felt deep sadness in her. I hoped she wouldn't say anything so that the girls would not hear her accent. I knew I would be in for a hard time there over that. It was time to say goodbye. Mother was crying, she kissed me. Hugged me. 'We'll write to you. And you write to us if you need anything.' And they left. I was surrounded by the girls straightaway. They continued taking me round and told me all sorts of things and showed me all kinds of things. They said they would show me how to write and read. 'Oh yes, please,' I said enthusiastically, hungrily.

They showed me Braille. One of the girls wrote out the alphabet and the numbers. They lent me a little frame to write with. Very quickly I learnt the alphabet. They found me a little book with words and sentences and helped me to read. They helped me to write. Within a day or two I had mastered the alphabet and started to read. They couldn't believe it. The news went round. Everybody knew that I had learned the alphabet and could read and write already. 'Isn't she clever? Well, she's from Teheran. Teheranis are all intelligent,' they commented. They had forgotten that I was a Turk.

CHAPTER THIRTEEN

I had arrived during the summer holidays. Another month and a half to go before school. The girls found me a copy of Book One. I read it, and I wrote out the dictations and they gave me Book Two. I got through that pretty quickly. And then Book Three. I finished that before school started. They were amazed. They talked to the teachers and told them with excitement, 'Monir can read and write and can read books One, Two, Three, and she's done all the dictation. We dictated to her.' The girls who were helping me were themselves on Grades Five, Six and coming on to Grade Seven. I couldn't wait for school to start.

The girls knew a little English, but they all spoke a broken Farsi which matched the broken Farsi the staff spoke. I thought it was very funny. Each time they spoke with Mama it was in broken Farsi. I giggled. 'She speaks broken Farsi because she doesn't know Farsi well but why do you speak broken Farsi?' I kept asking. 'Yes, because that's the Farsi she knows. If we speak properly she wouldn't understand,' they kept reminding me. 'Oh, pidgin Farsi.' Soon they had me labelled as serious, hard working and a good listener – they would bring all their troubles to me.

School opened. I had to start from Grade One. But because I knew it so well within a month I had passed to Grade Two. In another month I had passed on to Grade Three and at the end of the month I had started on Grade Four. They couldn't believe it. I had worked so fast in the six weeks of the summer holidays. I spent three months in Grade Four and another three months in Grade Five. By the end of that academic year I had completed five grades. It was a record.

Some of the girls started to feel uncomfortable. I had attained some of their levels and yet they'd been studying for a few years. The following summer holiday I wanted to study Grade Six. The teachers agreed, seeing my determination and insistence. A tutor was set aside to help me. I completed successfully, passing examinations with the Department of State Education. I started on Grade Seven straightaway. I had to go outside to school since the Blind School only went up to Grade Six, after which we were supposed to go out to a state school with sighted pupils. It had to be a Christian school and the only Christian school in the town was a school for Armenians so it had to be that. 'A whole year, nine months, one grade?' I kept saying. 'Surely I can do it quickly.' I had to do it that way, I was told. By the end of that year I had completed Grade Seven and during the summer I studied Grade Eight. They agreed to that only after a long discussion. 'It's too much for you,' they kept saying, 'You haven't taken any break in these two years you've been here. It's bad for you studying all the time. Day and night.'

'There are other things in the world besides studying,' Mama told me. Her caring voice is still in my ears.

'But I have missed out so much, there is so much catching up to do. I must, I love it.'

They agreed. By the end of summer I passed Grade Eight. I started Grade Nine straightaway, returning to the Armenian school. It seemed so slow, that nine months. By the end of it I passed. From now on, I was told, I had to spend a year on each grade, Ten, Eleven and Twelve because they were difficult. I could see that as well. I was to go to the best girls' school in the town with another girl who had been there many years, Laleh. Laleh wasn't happy with me at all. I had reached her level too quickly. I was her rival. How dare I?

At Grade Ten the choice was one of three areas: maths (mainly arithmetic), medicine (mainly physiology, biology and some maths), or literature (history and literature). Laleh and I had to study literature, the assumption being that we could not cope with the other two areas because they were very visual. I was to study the history of philosophy, history, Farsi literature, geography, a little bit of maths, and biology.

There were no books available in Braille for these grades. No blind person had reached these grades before. We had to transcribe books as we went along. In the evenings and weekends someone dictated from them and we transcribed them into Braille — a waste of our time and energy I thought. I had unlimited appetite and an intense urge for learning, 'There is so much to learn,' I kept saying to myself.

CHAPTER FOURTEEN

Letter to Miss D:
I am writing to tell you about your evil deeds of the past.
With this letter, I want to hand over the deep sense of
guilt and responsibility which I have been carrying
almost a quarter of a century. It is time now to hand it
back to you. It belongs to you. The guilt and
responsibility for your deeds has crushed me, suffocated
me, destroyed me all this time, crippled me. I am
handing it back to you. It is time for you to take it on.
You take it back. You deal with it. You carry it. It is yours.
Back to you.

In this period I made a very painful discovery which made me extremely unhappy. One of the senior staff, I shall call her Miss D, had what I thought was a special relationship with me. She loved me, I thought. I was her special girl. She was like a mother to me, I thought. She used to cuddle me. To begin with I liked it, as I had never been cuddled. Gradually this increased, intensified. She used to kiss me passionately. Some nights she used to come late, creeping into my room and stay with me a while or sometimes she took me to her room during the day whenever she had the time. It felt strange when she rubbed herself against me, especially the vaginal area, it didn't seem natural, it didn't feel right, but I did not protest. I liked the cuddles and thought that I was her special girl.

> You used me, abused me. I was vulnerable, needy. You understood that and you used that to use me. You had power over me. I looked up to you. I had taken refuge in there, in you, in the Blind School — my only hope. You knew that. You used me for your own ends. You made me feel that you loved me. That I was special to you. I believed that. I trusted that. I trusted you. I was hungry for that. To be loved. To be accepted. I had been searching for it all my life. Searching desperately. Love and acceptance, something I never had experienced and I would give anything in the world to get.

> In return, you asked me for sexual pleasure and I gave it. It seemed a small price to pay for my needs, love and acceptance. I gave it unquestioningly, unreservedly. You used me whenever you could, wherever you could, and however you wanted. All was in your power, in your control.

> You would creep into my room late in the night and you would touch me, caress me, hold me. I felt warmth, love, acceptance in those touches. You would kiss me, long deep kisses, rub yourself against me. Your face old, creased unattractive, would rub against mine, which was young, innocent, needy. You would begin holding my hands tight and rubbing me with your fingers and you

would gradually bring your face close and rub it against mine. And at times during the day would take me to your room and carry on there.

I remember the feel of your hideous face and your hideous voice, your hideous large body, your hideous laughter, your hysterical screams. The way you would lose your temper with us, which was often, stamping your feet, crying, screaming out in your hideous voice, which terrified us and made us guilty for having anything to do with your outburst.

Your rationalization, that you behaved in this manner because your father used to beat you up, only counted as a blackmail to us. Whatever happened, whatever you do, we must not protest, question, or hesitate, as this might provoke you. We had to put up with your unreasonable demands, behaviour, expectations.

Miss D was in her late forties. She was temperamental. She would get bursts of anger, stamp her feet, scream at the top of her voice, cry hysterically. This would happen often. Everyone knew they should be careful of not upsetting Miss D. She was called 'aunt'. All the staff were called aunts, apart from Mama, the person in charge. Staff changed occasionally, and numbers would vary from four to eight at a time.

We had to be on constant watch.

'Be careful, not a nice word about so-and-so in front of Miss D, she doesn't like it. She'll soon find an excuse to throw a temper,' we reminded each other, and warned newcomers. If one of us did provoke you, we would get stick from the other girls.

Miss D would talk about her past, how her mother had died when she was little and how her father had been brutal to her and beat her and that was why she lost her temper so easily and cried so much, and was so angry. The girls would feel sorry for her.

> I remember on one occasion you said you were sorry that
> you were doing this with me. I did not understand what
> you meant. I said, 'I don't mind.' You said, 'You know
> that I don't mind but you *do* mind.' I did not understand
> what you meant.
>
> Then I thought, maybe you thought on religious
> grounds that what you were doing to me was wrong. This
> was a sin. Anything to do with sex was a sin. But I did not
> have any feelings on religious grounds so I forgot all
> about it. I wondered what you could have meant.
> You used Latifeh as well.

One particular girl, Latifeh, was also known as her 'special girl'. It was well known that Miss D would go and spend hours with her. Things somehow didn't connect, make sense to me. Something was odd, unnatural.

Latifeh was small, petite, serious. She spoke quietly. She was about fourteen or fifteen. She had been there for a long time, since she was a little girl. She went round in a daze, had no particular interests, spoke good English. She did not like studying, or doing anything else for that matter, knitting or any handicraft.

She did not mix with girls much either. When we talked to her, either she did not hear us, or it took her a long time to respond. The girls would make fun of her. 'Oh, you are not here, are you? We can say anything about you, in front of you, and you won't even hear it.' She just wasn't there. 'In a world of dreams you are,' the girls would say, 'you are never with us.' She was a loner, she never liked socializing with anyone, did not have anything in common with anyone.

> With me, it happened as a teenager. But with Latifeh you
> had used her since she was a little girl, from what I

understood. As a result, she was confused, distorted, strange; she was never there herself, she was disturbed, distorted.

Quite often she was late for meals or prayers. 'Where have you been, Latifeh?' they would demand. 'Nowhere, I have been in my room, on my bed.' She would sit on her bed for hours, quietly, no one knew what she was thinking about. She would talk to herself occasionally, whispering. She would laugh or smile, or be unhappy, all on her own.

At times she looked distorted, disturbed, disoriented, would not respond, would not recognize anyone, she was in her own world all to herself. She would withdraw for periods into a complete silence, she was strange. Those periods the girls would avoid her, she was considered 'queer'. She would behave childishly at times, would giggle at something which others did not find funny. She did not have any desire for anything. At times she would look as though she had no life in her, did not care whatever happened around her.

It took me a long time to understand why she was the way she was. She had been abused for a very long time, deceived, tricked. She had no family that anyone knew of. We did not know anything about her past. How did she come to be there? We did not know. She was quiet, dull.

You started by holding my hand, rubbing it with your fingers and watching my face, for a response to that facial comfort, that warmth on my face. Then you would proceed, getting closer to me, putting your arms around me, hugging me, putting your face against mine, looking into my face. You would hold my hand for a long period, evoking in me a sense of relaxation, comfort, warmth and at the same time you would watch my face. Then you would go further, rubbing your face against mine and that would go on for some time, then you would rub my body and touch my body and caress it, the more you did so the more relaxed I would become.

Then you would go a stage further, rub yourself against me, against my body and the lower part of your body against mine. You would kiss, deep kisses, rubbing yourself against me. I remember you taking me to your bathroom and doing it there for a long period until I was exhausted.

One day, just after lunch, I remember the maids wanted you, they kept calling you. They knew you were there and I think they knew I was with you, and maybe they knew what you were up to. They kept calling. You ignored them and carried on with what you were doing. At some point I felt that one of them was just about to come in. You still didn't leave me, you carried on regardless. I was alarmed. Did you know how they would respond, how the word would go round, how others would view me? It was very alarming.

You left it all to me. You loaded all the anxieties on to me. You thought you had power over the maids, so that they would not talk about it or challenge you. You could scream at them using any excuse you wished. You could stamp your feet and scream at the top of your voice, or, you could even sack them. They did not want that so they would keep quiet. And no matter for what urgent reason they needed you, they left us and you carried on until you had had enough and let me go.

It went on and on and on and on. Only when you had had enough, only then, you let me go, exhausted.

Your large body would shake when you were doing it and I never understood why. I used to be puzzled over this. 'Why does she shake' I would say to myself. You would tremble, shake, all over. I knew you were doing the same to Latifeh and maybe she knew that you did it to me as well.

You did try it on other girls as well. At times they would talk about your wet kisses and prolonged holding of their hands and they would laugh and giggle and mock you for it. Maybe you tried everyone, to seek out the most vulnerable. We found refuge in you.

I gave in to your needs in the hope and expectation that I was special to you, that you loved me, that you chose me.

You stopped eventually with me after a couple of years when you discovered my deep disappointment and disenchantment with you and your behaviour. But I am sure you carried on doing it to Latifeh.

A member of staff complained that I'd been rude and demanded a public apology. I had merely answered her back, but it was in front of others and her pride was at stake. Miss D said I had to apologize or be thrown out of the school. The bell was rung. Everyone was gathered in the hall and I apologized.

If Miss D really loved me, if I really was her special girl, why did she force me to do this and threaten to send me home?

I felt that what you did to me was the ultimate expression of your love towards me, of your care, of your concern. I felt like believing that you only did it to me, that you only chose me. When eventually I realized that I was not special to you, that you did not have any love towards me, I was devastated. It shattered me. I felt I was used, abused. You had power over me, you manipulated me. I was angry with myself for being so naïve to have fallen into your trap. I felt I was stupid for not having recognized your intentions, your true intentions. I felt that the fault lay in me. Why did I not stop you doing what you did to me? What did I do to attract you? I felt wicked.

On one occasion over something trivial, I lost my temper. I started shouting and screaming and banging the doors. I was shaking all over. They carried me upstairs, they got a doctor to check me over. 'It's exhaustion, she's been working too hard,' was their verdict. 'We knew we shouldn't have let you study so intensely,' said the staff, 'you must take it easy.' I could not talk to anyone about Miss D. I was too ashamed, guilty, confused, I bottled it up and it burned me inside.

Now I understand why I became so deeply unhappy when you left the country for a holiday in England. I felt you had deserted me, that you had forsaken me. It was like a mother leaving the baby she was deeply attached to. I would cry and cry.

I became ill at some point and was taken to hospital and kept in there for a while. I felt nothing was right without her around. The world had stopped for me. Life had stopped. Breathing at a standstill. I saw nothing around me but misery, depression. I felt nothing but unhappiness. I thought of nothing, but you. I could not understand why you had left me. My mother had left me!

I behaved like a child that did not want separation and exhibited all the symptoms of a traumatic separation from another. A loving, caring mother.

Miss D would have men friends as well, would take them to her bedroom. One in particular, a young accountant much younger than herself. It went on for some time with him and, later, with another member of the staff, a woman. They became lovers quite openly. They would cuddle in the candlelight, looking deep into each other's eyes. The maids would see them and tell us. We could feel it in their voices, the way they talked to each other, seductive.

When once I complained that she had not come to see me when I was ill, she said, 'I came several times, you weren't in your room.' I wasn't in my room? She should not have gone away without seeing me, checking me. She had given me high expectations. She did not understand what she had got herself caught up in. She did not understand what kind of mess she had got me into.

The thought that I was special had led me to high expectations. I needed her to respond to my demands, to my needs. If I was not well, I wanted her to come and spend time with me, bring me drinks, pay me attention, the attention that I desperately needed and I felt I was justified to expect from her after what I was giving to her.

I mixed up love with sexual needs. I thought that she cared for me and that was the way she expressed it. I did not realize that this did not have any relation towards the emotions. She was using my body only. This painful realization came to me gradually. It was as though the whole world had collapsed around me. Everything had stopped for me. My life energy was trapped, could not flow any longer.

What was it about me that made her choose me? Was I dirty and horrible now? How naïve I was to be tricked. How stupid I was for not having recognized her intentions. Why did I not protest? How could I have allowed this to happen to me?

What did I do to deserve it? Was I basically bad? That bad, to bring this rejection upon myself as well as the past rejections and accusations. There must be something in me which made them, Miss D and my mother, do these things to me. What could it be? Was it some evil power in me, the one I took to my father, the very one mother often spoke about which brought them bad luck? I must be the one causing these events.

I dreamed mother's death. My dream occurred the night she died. At four o'clock in the morning, which was the precise time of her death. I was in my third year at the Blind School, it was a winter's night.

In my dream mother, myself, and my older brother, were travelling in a car out into the country. It was night, it was dark. There, we got out of the car. Mother seemed a bit strange. She was attacked by a wolf. The wolf leapt at her throat. And there she died of her wound. I learned later that an incision had been made in mother's throat to aid her breathing.

The evil power and stupidity on my part must have been at the core of it. I was convinced. The same bad power in me that had enabled me to dream my mother's death on the very night she died and my father's death just before he died. The evil aspect of myself was responsible for these events. I had learned as a child that anyone who foretold future unhappiness and misfortune ought to be avoided. I ought to be avoided.

This experience made me hate women and myself for being a woman.

> You took advantage of my innocence, my vulnerability, my neediness, of my intense need for security, love and acceptance. My own home had rejected me! My own mother had rejected me. The acceptance, for which I had been searching all my life, I never had experienced.
>
> You well knew how needy and vulnerable I was. Innocent. Needy. You used that knowledge for your own wicked ends, for your own satisfaction. It is pitiful, your wretchedness. Or maybe not. You deserve it. What you did to me. You put me through hell.

CHAPTER FIFTEEN

The head teacher of the state school was a hard woman. Reluctantly she had agreed that blind students attend the school. 'All right, we'll see how they get on shall we?' she had said after a lengthy negotiation with the missionaries. We were exempt from religious education, and physical education, and special arrangements were made for us to be taught maths. Once, over an exam arrangement, she commented: 'Why don't these girls stay home and learn basket work of some sort instead of being such a nuisance?' This was reported to us. With us she hardly interacted. She completely ignored us. We did not exist in that school, did not belong there, as far as she was concerned.

In that school most of the teachers were disillusioned, disappointed, demoralized, embittered, angry. Some were old and out of date in their teaching methods. One teacher couldn't at times distinguish one pupil from another. His eyes were closed, he appeared to sleep most of the time. When he called someone up to read, the girls would say, 'You go today instead of me.' One teacher, a young biology teacher, was different: she was enthusiastic, full of energy. Though she was a medical student, most of the time she talked politics: 'the more people are paid, the more they are meant to serve the people,' she would say. The girls liked her. Her classes were lively. She was brave, honest, outspoken. Everything she said made sense. 'Women have to learn to fight together if we are to be freed.' We did more politics with her than biology. 'What if she's reported?' the girls would ask. 'How do we know she's not a government spy?' Many girls kept quiet in the discussions but everyone listened with great interest. 'If she's for real, the secret police would have got her by now. She must be a spy,' the speculation would go.

Some of the unfriendliness and hostility we encountered from the teachers at the state school was because we came from the missionary school and missionaries were known to be firm supporters of the government. Church prayers were always said for the royal family. The bishop would pray for the royal family passionately. For the Shah and his family especially. For the crown prince. For the queen. For the Shah's sisters and brothers. For the queen's parents and relatives. For their friends and so on. For the people in the army and high positions. For the mayors of the cities. Especially Isfahan. Asking the Lord for blessing, protection. Asking for long life for them. Especially for the Shah. Wishing them all happiness, good luck, and thanking the Lord for

their existence and for their goodwill and for their care towards
all of us.

On some special occasions they would invite government
officials to the church. Then passions would heat up. Princess
Ashraf would visit the school occasionally as she was the patron,
and the Shah once paid a visit when Queen Elizabeth visited Iran.
They visited the Blind School together.

Three days before the visit, hundreds of security people came
to the school and stayed the whole time until the visit was over.
Everything had to be watched. They were all over, on the roofs, in
the buildings, around the buildings, all armed. It was a tense,
anxious time.

The story went round that the bishop was a spy; he had
betrayed his country, his people; he was a traitor, he was on the
side of evil. Strong feelings were expressed against him,
especially by the young people, the sighted students, young
teachers.

At the Blind School one collective feeling filled the air. We
were uncivilized savages, the wretched of the earth. Our families
had abandoned us. Our country had forsaken us. The missionaries had taken mercy on us with the intention of saving our
souls. Had it not been for them we would have died out on the
streets from hunger and diseases. We had to be grateful and
obedient. It was the least we could do.

There was a discrepancy between the homely, family image,
which the Blind School projected, and its treatment of us, the
pupils, as outsiders, foreign, strange. We were not supposed to
bother the staff, and our 'aunts' — in the lunch hour, or at tea
break, or rest hour or whenever they were having a day off. In our
experience, mothers and aunties did not take days off, nor did
they feed us with one thing and eat some other food themselves.
The staff did not eat with us. Our foods were not good for their
stomachs, they said. 'Iranian food is strange, funny,' the younger
ones told us. They holidayed separately from us, they ate
separately, but above all it was their blame which hurt: 'Your own

people don't care for you. Had it not been for us you would have been out on the streets.' Like a stab it went through the heart. 'But you're our aunties. This is a home. We are one family. You keep telling us.'

The staff did not use our style of toilets with no seats. Our style was to squat. By squatting down one exerted pressure on the muscles, making it easier for the body to expel. Medically this has been recognized as natural and healthy. You don't wipe yourself with paper, but wash yourself with water. In each of our lavatories there was a tap and an *aftabeh*, a special container with a spout. We did not have European baths. We had showers. They did not like our music. We loved music. Music and poetry were part of our everyday existence. The country people who do not have an education learn poetry by heart and all our experience and knowledge is in the poetry. We quoted from it to prove a point, to emphasize, to illustrate.

There was a youth club at the church and a Sunday school, neither of which we attended. Only sighted people. We weren't good enough, we thought.

The girls were greatly interested in boys. Having a boyfriend had great prestige, an achievement. We were allowed to make friends with boys, see them, talk with them, provided it was done all in public. We should sit with them where people could see us, otherwise people could talk and they did not want the Blind School to get a bad name. In the past one of the older girls had become pregnant. They did not want such a thing to be repeated.

Boyfriends, sex, were hot talking points among the girls. Mr M had confided in a couple of the girls and told them what it was like. He was a young teacher. He talked to them about his experience with prostitutes. It went round. Everyone talked about it and giggled. Everyone was told and told not to tell anyone.

The young sighted girls who worked at the school, either Iranian or British trainees, were allowed to go out with boys. This created resentment among the others. 'If they can go out, why not us? They are the same age as we are. It's not fair, they know what to do and we don't.'

Farideh and I, as the only two blind girls at the state school, had to study together. That was one way we overcame the reading problem. Farideh was not happy with me at all. I had reached her level too quickly. She'd been in the limelight and now I occupied that place. She'd been at the missionary school since childhood and she spoke excellent English. Resentment which had been building up for some time in the Blind School reached a peak. The girls hated me. 'She's obsessed with learning. She takes so much of the staff's attention. They arrange special things for her. She's forgotten she's only a Turk. She arranges reading sessions with people, she gets sighted people to read to her, separately, privately, whatever next?'

They were egged on by Safieh who was in her late twenties and had been at the missionary school since childhood but who did not apply herself to her studies. She had power over the other girls, she turned them easily whichever way she wanted. No one dared to disagree with her. Everyone followed her completely and she was my major enemy. She was very interested in boys, totally preoccupied with them. She had no family. No one knew anything about her background. Many girls were alone like that. They had no information about their background. One girl knew her mother, who was a prostitute, and very occasionally they met secretly. She was a disturbed girl, angry, bitter, temperamental, and Safieh used her a lot against the ones she did not like, and against me. Life became very difficult for me. I was nervous they might actually attack me. I kept to myself. Yet I had to eat with the others, in the dining room, and go to prayers and so on. The staff caught on eventually and put me in a room on my own, downstairs, away from the others. They began to walk in groups outside my door, swearing at me and calling me names.

I began to make new friends, with the sighted girls at the state school. The girls were intrigued to know how I coped with everyday things. Sometimes they said things like: 'How do you manage to eat when you can't see?' to which I replied: 'Do you put a mirror in front of you when you are eating? How do you know where your mouth is?' We also learned together. They read things out to me and I explained them, as I had before I went to the missionary school. This made Safieh more jealous. I made more friends than she did. She wasn't very interested in learning for its own sake as long as she passed her exams, that was enough for her, and she did not like my having so many other friends.

They would compete as to who would be my friend. 'She reads it once and she understands and explains to me. I don't understand and I've read it many times,' they would say laughingly. 'She's just so clever. I feel stupid compared with her.' Comments like this embarrassed me. I did not really believe what they said. I felt they were saying it just to make me happy, to make me feel that I was not wasting their time, that they were getting something out of it too. To me it seemed always that they were the givers, they were giving all the time, and I was the taker. I did not feel that I reciprocated.

My new friends invited me home to meet their families. I loved talking to their brothers. I enjoyed talking with young men. I thought of them as intelligent because they were men. Men were intelligent, the opposite of women. Women were only interested in petty things, I thought. Men saw me as intellectual and they respected me. 'This girl has a good mind, this friend of yours,' they would comment. I discussed books with them: Charles Dickens, Victor Hugo, Shakespeare. I had listened to Shakespeare on the radio. I was reading Charlotte Brontë and Jane Austen in English as well as Farsi literature including Molavi, the Sufi writer. I recited poetry and talked about it. Sometimes one of them would record my talks. There would be silence while I talked. It would go on for a long time. Their fascination encouraged me to do more. I felt happy, satisfied, pleased with myself, the sessions seemed to confirm my existence, the young men approved of me, affirmed me. I loved the visits. My girlfriends were taken aback. 'How come you know so much?' Although I was blind their brothers seemed to respect me more than their sisters, the girls thought. But as friends we needed one another. I needed them to read to me, and they needed me to understand and explain the lessons. But our friendships became somewhat strained.

CHAPTER SIXTEEN

Sometimes I visited Mama's office at the Blind School, when Mama would be doing things and she would chat to me occasionally. One day I noticed the typewriter on the desk, and I fiddled around with it. 'Is this how you type? You put all your fingers on these keys?'

'Yes,' Mama said, 'I'll show you. S D F A and so on.'

'Can I have a piece of paper?'

'Yes, I'll put it in for you.' She did. I typed while she carried on. After a while she came over. 'Let me see how you're getting on. Good girl, you've done very well. It's correct, you've done beautifully. You've even written some words. "As", "lad", "sad". Shall I show you the next row?'

'Yes, please,' I begged excitedly. She did.

'This is "R". You press with your index finger without lifting the other fingers,' and so on. 'I have to go upstairs for something but you can stay in the office and type if you like.'

It was great. I typed away memorizing all the letters she'd shown me and making up words. I kept hoping she would stay away, giving me a chance to practise longer. She came back, 'Let's see what you have done. This is brilliant, everything is correct. I tell you what, I'll get someone to teach you the rest. You can type.'

'When?' I demanded.

'Tomorrow? I will see,' she laughed. 'But I will do it, I promise. You are very good. I am impressed.'

That night I was excited. I kept memorizing all the letters in my head. I could type. I couldn't wait for my typing sessions that were organized for the next few days. I mastered typing quickly. I would sit and type pages and pages, anything, making things up, stories, anecdotes, translations of Farsi, little stories and take them to show someone. 'Is this right?' They read, and laughed. 'This is very good, you are doing very well.' They showed my typing to the bishop. 'Monir learned this in such a short time, it all happened so quickly, we can't believe it.' They asked me to type when people came to have a look round the school — this happened often, tourists or anyone passing through. The place was open for visits at any time. The school wanted attention and publicity.

I asked whether I could learn Farsi typing. 'I would love to type my own letters,' I said. We always dictated our letters, which was far from satisfactory. When I wrote to someone, I was always conscious that I had to hurry up, I was holding the writer back or taking up her time, so the words didn't come out quite right or the letter did not say enough. Now, I could do my own letters, take as long as I liked and write whatever I liked, in whatever form, without worrying about making a mistake, or the writer laughing at me or sounding bored, telling me I should hurry up. 'Well, we shall have to make inquiries,' Mama said, 'the school hasn't got a Farsi typewriter. But I don't see why we shouldn't buy one if you're interested. You'll have to go outside though to learn it. I don't know where we can find anyone to teach you.'

'I'll find out,' I said, 'if you let me learn, I'll find out where and how.' I enquired at the state school and found an evening class. I rang them. 'You are blind and yet you want to learn to type?' the man on the phone answered in surprise.

'Yes, but look, I can type English already.'

'I can't see how this can be done,' he went on, as though he hadn't heard what I had just said.

'But look, I can type English you know. I can actually type. In English you see.'

'Type English?' he repeated. It took a while for him to take it in. In the end, though, he reluctantly agreed to let me have a go.

Soon I went to the class. The tutor knew I was coming but didn't know what to make of me. I was seated at a desk with a typewriter in front of me. 'There are many people here,' he said, 'I can't give you much attention but just see what you can do. Now everybody, put your fingers on the keys of the second row leaving two keys in the middle. I am coming round to check everybody. No, this is not right, you must put your fingers like this,' he said to someone. I knew where to place my fingers, that was all right, I thought. 'No, no, you have to leave this key free, just relax your fingers,' he went all round. It took him a long time to come back to me. 'That's right, your fingers are all right. Now I'll show you which fingers go on which keys, let me put some paper in for you.' I had explored the typewriter earlier. As he picked up the paper I took it from him and put it into the typewriter, straight. 'That's beautiful,' he said, in a relaxed voice. He put his finger on my left small finger, 'This is *shin*.' Next he touched *sin*, and the next *yeh*, and so on. 'Now can you press those for me?' One by one I did. 'Very good. What is the first one?'

'*Shin*,' I said.

'Next one?'

'*Sin*.'

'Next one?'

'*Yeh*.'

'Very good, and the other way, yes that's very good. Keep practising them,' and then he turned and talked to the others while I practised. In a few weeks I learned Farsi typing and the Blind School bought a Farsi typewriter. I couldn't believe it. No one could believe it.

I started writing. I would sit for hours typing long letters to friends in Teheran. My letters would come to ten, fifteen pages, tightly spaced to save paper. I found penfriends in other towns. A new world had opened to me. I could talk, communicate. I was 'the first blind girl in the country to learn Farsi typing'. The school kept telling all the visitors, 'Look what the school is capable of. She types both, English and Farsi.' I was put on show more often now. This made me feel uncomfortable, but it was a small price to pay. 'We never thought you would master Farsi typing,' the class teacher told me. 'English is very simple compared with Farsi, you see. We are proud of having taught you.'

I had indeed found learning Farsi typing harder than I'd anticipated. In Farsi there are thirty-three letters, for some letters there are three different symbols, so on the typewriter there are three keys for one letter, depending on the position of the letter in the word, whether it comes at the beginning, in the middle or at the end of the word and whether it joins on to the preceding letter. For some letters there are two or three types, for example, three types of S and two types of H; this is the result of mixing Farsi with Arabic. I had one major difficulty with Farsi typing, to learn which letters join on to each other and which don't — this was difficult, especially as I had no visual picture of the script.

One of the families mother had worked for in Teheran had a young daughter, a school teacher who had since become a close friend of mine. I did not see much of her when we lived there because she was quite a bit older than me, and she worked hard, but when I moved to Isfahan and went to school and started writing letters to her, we became friends.

I typed long, long letters to Oteghe, this young school teacher. Whenever I went for a holiday back to Teheran I visited her. She told me that she read my letters out to her class to show them how to express themselves in writing. I was surprised and upset. I begged her not to do that ever again. I said, 'If you do it again, I won't write you letters any more.'

'But why?' she asked. 'What is it that you don't like about me reading your letters to my students? They are sixteen, seventeen years old and all girls you know.'

'I can't tell you why but I beg you not to do it again. I won't write to you again if you do it.'

'No, I won't do it if it upsets you,' she said, 'I promise. But I wish you could tell me why.'

I could not tell her why. The truth was that I did not feel my letters were worthy of being read out to a classroom of teenagers who were much better educated than I was. I felt maybe they'd make fun of my letters. I could not believe my letters were good enough to read out to a class of seventeen-year-old girls from educated parents, middle-class girls who would become teachers or go on to university. In no way could I see my letters would be good enough for them.

When I went to Teheran I sometimes stayed overnight in Oteghe's room. Oteghe put a mattress on the floor for me. Sometimes she asked, 'Do you want to sleep on my bed? I'll sleep on the floor.'

'Oh no. No way,' I would say, 'I like sleeping on the floor.' Such consideration was too much for me. At mealtimes they laid a tablecloth on the floor in the hall, as was the custom, on which the food was to be served. We would all sit round it to eat. I would sit with them but mother, who was working for the family, would only eat in the kitchen. She did not want to come and sit with everyone else. She did not feel that she was good enough to eat with them. She kept saying she liked to eat on her own in the kitchen and they did not press her to join them. I was embarrassed. I felt I wasn't doing things right, not quite right. Maybe I was not holding the spoon properly, or using the fork exactly as I should. They tried hard to make me feel at home. They were kindly, unpretentious people. There was Oteghe, my friend the schoolteacher, her mother, her sister who was married with two children, and her husband, a lawyer, who always joked and tried to make me laugh. They tried hard to get through to me, and to make me feel comfortable, at ease, one of them, but the reality was that I could not be one of them. I was not one of them. I had not grown up with their experiences, my past experiences were totally different, my life had been totally different. We had few points in common. We liked each other, respected each other, accepted each other. They tried hard to make me feel one of them, not to feel like an outsider, but I did feel like an outsider. I was an outsider. I was not on their level, not from their class, and I was not at ease with their high standard of comfortable living.

I wanted to write a long story. I had to do it in Braille so that I could have access to it. Every evening I would carry my Braille typewriter over to the school building and write until the bell went for prayer. 'Couldn't I continue? Do I have to go to prayers?' My mind was not there anyway, when I was at prayers. I would write as words passed my mind. The story developed, contrasting the rich and the poor, the powerful and the powerless, the evil and the good. As I finished each page, I piled it in a bundle. It was getting thicker every day. It was coming on. I had a long way to go yet. There just wasn't enough time in twenty-four hours for all the things I wanted to do.

'What about my violin? I don't have time to practise.' I had picked up the violin over the last two years and I was doing well. I was the first violinist in the school orchestra. We gave concerts at Christmas, Easter, at the end of term. Any excuse was seized upon for throwing a party, inviting the élite of the town, showing what the school was capable of. Hundreds of people would fill the hall, including the mayor, the schoolmasters, the prominent army officers stationed locally. If any member of the royal family visited the town, the school was always included. Another occasion for a party or ceremony.

When one of the boys, named Murad, died after a very long illness, and they carried his body out of the building, I wanted to write about it. I wrote about his death, his illness and the way it had affected the school. 'That's a very good story,' the school authorities said with surprise when I read it to them. After some discussion they decided to take me to see the bishop, the Iranian bishop.

That evening in the bishop's house I read out my story. He was known as a literary man and his sermons were regarded as the best in the country. 'It's very good, excellent.'

'Should I make any changes?' I asked.

'I don't think so. It can stand as it is.'

It was decided that I would read it at the end-of-term ceremony. I had to practise. Important people, hundreds of people, would be there.

'Now Monir is going to read a story she's written herself,' I heard the announcement. I don't know how I read but somehow I did. I heard the applause. I was sweating and shaking.

'We are very proud of you,' Mama said to me afterwards. 'You give the school a very good name.' People kept going up to her and saying things like, 'you have got very clever girls.' This made me think of writing a play for the next ceremony.

I had a play ready for the Christmas party. I directed it, and I acted in it. It went down well. The applause went on for some time. After the play I had to play the violin with the orchestra. I was exhausted. I was too shaky. with excitement, exhaustion.

The bishop's wife invited me to stay with them one weekend. 'It will give you a chance to rest,' she said. I felt very important. Being invited for a weekend in the bishop's house. I couldn't believe it. What do I do now? I wondered, as I was left in the spare room all on my own. I explored the place. I had a private bathroom and for the first time I used a *farangi* (European toilet) — from abroad, exotic. I didn't know what to do with the toilet paper and I threw it at the back, to my embarrassment later — I was frightened of doing something wrong. Surely I should not flush it down, it might block the toilet, I thought. I was anxious not to do anything wrong and wrong I did, throwing the paper on the floor for the bishop's wife to see. They had a cook, maids, chauffeur, a washerwoman, waiters, the lot. They had a summer house in the country. The bishop's wife was kind to me, but I couldn't talk to them. I was anxious, conscious of being out of place, the system wasn't happy with me, just as I wasn't comfortable with the system, with the people. I wasn't one of them, I wasn't a Christian. 'Not yet,' they said, hoping that one day I would become a Christian, be baptized, rescued, saved as they saw it.

Every morning at prayers we were each asked: 'What is your greatest ambition in the world?' and the right answer was: 'To be baptized as a Christian one day' — that person was highly praised and prayed for. 'To be given wisdom and guidance to do the right thing at the right time, the Lord's will, one day we all should pray for her.' This answer never came from me, to their great disappointment. They decided to arrange a special tutor to teach me religion. Private tuition once a week. It was decided and fixed without asking me. I was told after they made the arrangements with the best tutor in the town, Miss A, who ran a private boarding school for the girls of the town's élite. She spoke good Farsi, was highly educated. It was taking me too long, I had to be helped along and Miss A was the right person. She would satisfy my doubts. The sessions started. She would read a text and then we talked about it and she let me ask questions. 'When Jesus says, "If someone slaps you on the face on one side, turn the other cheek," what does he mean?'

'It just means that you forgive your enemies.'

'But why? If someone slaps me on my face on one side, I wouldn't turn the other; I'd feel like slapping them back.'

'But that isn't Christian-like.'

I could not forget how Miss D had threatened me with expulsion and forced me to apologize publicly, yet I did not think I had done wrong. That was unfair punishment, not Christian, I said to myself. They went for some time, these sessions, and we weren't getting anywhere. She gave up on me in the end. 'We can only pray that you'll see sense one day,' they said. I had to be true to myself, I felt strongly, I couldn't go along with it just to please them as most of the other girls did. Sohila was the only other pupil who had not converted to Christianity. Her family was a strong support. The staff thought the day would come and they kept praying for her. Nasreen was from Tabriz, the Turkish part of the country, and one of five children, all blind: she had three brothers who went to the boys' school run by the German missionaries, also in Isfahan, and a sister, who was also at the Blind School. Her family were well educated, politically aware. She talked about the corruption in the royal family, the poverty and injustice in the country, how women were oppressed, how the wealth of the country was wasted, and so on.

Nasreen was to be sent to England for teacher training, but I wanted to go to the university. It was unthinkable. No blind female had gone to university in Iran before. 'It doesn't mean that it can't be done,' I kept saying. I was in my final year at school preparing for the exams, hard work, but harder work was needed to convince the authorities that I could go to university. 'Please let me try,' I insisted.

'Why should you want to go to university? I didn't go to university,' the deputy head said to me.

I cried bitterly that night. 'If she didn't go that doesn't mean that I can't go,' I kept saying to myself. 'That's not a good reason.' I begged and pleaded. One night I couldn't get to sleep for crying. Aunt Irene, a Scotswoman, was on duty and came to my room. She was a kind, gentle, motherly woman. I talked to her. 'I'd love to go to university. I want to study psychology. I love learning. Why don't they let me?' She listened sympathetically, held my hands and wiped my tears. I knew that she had no power on the education side of the school, since she was responsible for household management. Maman was away on holiday and so was Miss D (who was in charge of education), while the new deputy head was not in favour of my university application. 'What on earth would you do afterwards?' she asked. 'You should try to learn something practical, with your hands.' I thought of the bishop, and of his wife who'd been supportive to me all along, in my writing, and I asked if they'd been consulted. The deputy head was silent. I could tell she did not know what to do. 'We'll think about it.'

The bishop agreed that I should sit the exam. He had said that it would be a credit to the school if I succeeded in the university entrance exam. The deputy head gave in.

For her this agreement was a costly one. She was a firm believer that a pupil, under no circumstances, should 'win' as she saw it. She was the 'loser'.

The university exams were set at a national level, and entrants were allowed two choices. I chose first Teheran University, subject: psychology, and second, Isfahan University, subject: psychology.

The results were announced in the national press. The day the results were announced, our maths teacher came in with the newspaper and started to read out the names.

My heart beat as though it would burst out of my chest any minute. My blood ran hot. After a bit, he said my name. 'Monir: accepted, Isfahan University and Teheran University.'

'Are you sure? Is it my name? You're not making it up? Are you seeing it properly?'

'Yes, I am. Here it is, Monir.' The news was a bombshell.

That year, two thousand students had been accepted at a national level out of twenty thousand applicants, and I had been one of them. I had been accepted by both universities.

The staff, the ones who had taught me, were over the moon. It was their success, they had got me into university. Reporters appeared to take photos and talk to the authorities, 'How did you manage to get a blind girl through the entrance exam for Teheran University? It's the first time in the history of our country. A blind girl going to university?' It was their achievement, not mine. The staff had done it. The school had achieved it. The Blind School and the state school. It was their achievement, their success. It was as though I was incidental. The school received massive publicity. National papers splashed their front pages with the news, sensationalized it. *A Blind Girl passes University Entrance Exam for the first time in the Country* — and this blind girl was the product of Norain School for the Blind — everyone can see what the church has done for Iran, the British Anglican Church. What an achievement. It seemed the achievement wasn't mine, but that of the British church, the Anglican church, the Blind School of Norain. My life story was published in many versions, in many papers. *A Working Class Girl from Blind School Enters University. The Entire Schooling Done in Five Years and now Enters University, a Blind Working-Class Girl from Norain.*

I was bewildered, astonished, amazed by the sudden attention, from the media, radio, television, newspapers and magazines, the constant interviews and photo sessions. I did not know what to make of it. One minute having been told it was no good my applying to university, and the next minute being treated as the pride of the school.

The time had come for me to leave Norain, Isfahan. To move to Teheran to attend the university. And yet I had not become a Christian. I had failed them.

CHAPTER SEVENTEEN

Khadijeh, a junior lecturer at Teheran University, happened to visit the Blind School in Isfahan with her family during the summer holidays. Hearing of my choice — to study psychology at Teheran University — and my need for accommodation, she promised to help. On her return she had contacted the head of the accommodation section, Mrs Nasri, who had promised that a room would be reserved for me in the hall of residence, and that I need not worry. When I arrived I was told to wait for a while until there was accommodation available. Khadijeh, my kind-hearted friend, allowed me to stay with her until the situation was clarified. After two weeks we were told there was no place for me in the hall after all. Khadijeh, deeply disappointed on my behalf, said to the head of accommodation, 'But you did promise a room for her. What am I to tell her now? I feel I have failed her.' The head responded, 'What do you expect me to say? At the last minute a local mayor rings up and says, "Have a room ready for a friend's daughter." Do you expect me to say no to him and give the room to a blind girl?'

I was devastated at this explanation. Not just because I was stranded. Because of the way I was valued, measured. By 'blind girl' she had also meant a girl with no important connections. The missionaries hadn't used their connections with Princess Ashraf to secure a place for me. Because I had not become a Christian, they would only contact her on matters of importance, such as asking for donations or for favours for their own acquaintances.

Corruption was common in Iran. It happened at every level. If you wanted something done, it depended on whom you knew rather than what the need was.

I was asked to tea at the British ambassador's house. I did not know how to behave, what to say, what was appropriate in the company of ambassadorial ladies. I counted the minutes in my head, and sat there deaf and dumb as well as blind, hearing the refined voices and accents all around me, chattering away as on any other of their many coffee mornings. When the ambassador came in, I wished the ground would open up and swallow me. I did not understand why I was there, I felt like a puppet. It heightened and confirmed my experience as an outsider. I was confused, nervous, anxious, stressed. They were just as confused as I was. How could they communicate with a blind girl who wasn't even dressed properly, who didn't look or behave in any way like them?

This event was reported in the papers. *The Blind Girl Goes to Tea at the British Ambassador's House.* The report did not mention that I did not get my cup of tea because the ladies did not know how to communicate with me, how to tell me where my tea was, and I did not have the experience or confidence to ask.

During that time it seemed I had to perform. I had no control over my life — as to how many interviews I gave in a day, or what sort of things I should disclose, or withhold. I had no one to talk to, to get advice from, to share my fears, worries, concerns. I was alone. I did not know how to cope with the sudden fame.

The irony was that this suddenly famous person did not have anywhere to live, did not have the right study equipment, such as a typewriter, a tape-recorder, and so on; and did not have the money to pay her fees or her living costs. These questions were not asked by the media, but I would dwell internally on these questions.

I took a basement room in the house of a grocer opposite the first-years' college in desperation. He was an odd character, in his fifties. He was a hard, mean man. He had an attractive wife, and a daughter of about ten from his first marriage. I was told there were five or six rooms beautifully furnished in his house, locked all the time, except for the one room at the back of the shop, which they used, all three of them.

In the middle of the night he walked around from room to room, down to the other basement, carrying things, mixing things up. I would hear him stirring liquid and pouring it into various buckets. It was mysterious to me, threatening.

He had absolute power over his wife and his daughter. His wife was forbidden to leave the house and not allowed to speak to anybody, particularly to men. She left the house only when she visited *hamam*, the public bath house, once every ten days. She was a prisoner.

On one occasion an electrician came to do some work in the house. She sent me to ask him something. She was not allowed to talk to any man, she said, she had to cover herself and hide away. And yet, I felt she longed to talk to people, men especially.

I felt unsafe there, insecure, frightened. Every night I would lie awake, sometimes rigid with fear, thinking any minute he might enter my room in the basement. He was bitter, harsh, heartless.

I had to move out. I had been there six weeks and felt I could not go on living there. His suspicious activities in the night, all those locked rooms. One of them, I was told, had been his wedding room with his first wife. He had kept everything exactly as on the first night. No one was allowed to enter that room, nor any of the other rooms, except himself, and that he did in the night. It all seemed mysterious and suspicious. I was frightened to stay. I felt that place could break me.

With the help of a student, I found myself another room. I worked out how much rent I owed the shopkeeper and took the money to him. 'How much money do I owe you?' I asked. He told me a higher figure. 'But the figure I worked out is different,' I said. I added it again in front of him. 'Yes,' he said, agreeing with me in surprise. 'You have worked this out beforehand, haven't you?' he sneered.

My new room was in an American family's house about twenty minutes' walk to the college. Every day I walked to the college with a friend, a classmate whose name was Farideh. She took a bus to the house, and we walked from there together.

The American family was kind to me. They had two little children. The father was an anthropologist. There was deep suspicion among the people about these American anthropologists who seemed to be turning up everywhere in Iran. 'What are they up to? Who are they kidding?' people would comment. The family had many friends, also anthropologists.

Among the students there were feelings of distrust and suspicion of Americans and the British. Whoever associated with them, in their view, must be working for them.

Most of the girls were confused about me. They were suspicious of my occasional meetings with the British and American ladies connected to the mission. The Blind School kept in touch with me. I was their showcase, after all.

Some of the missionaries' friends in Teheran occasionally visited me and invited me for a meal, or for tea, or to spend a weekend in their luxurious villas. Some of these friends had connections with the court and with Princess Ashraf, the patron of the Blind School.

The girls wondered — was I a SAVAK agent? Did I spy on them? Why else would these ladies in their Rolls Royces visit me?

SAVAK was the National Intelligence and Security Organization.

Its agents were trained by the CIA and MOSAD, the Israeli Secret Police. Its duty was to inform on suspects and protect the Shah. Each group of students was supposed to have at least one SAVAK informer on board, both at home and abroad. SAVAK was an extremely large and powerful organization, with the Shah at its head. There was fear and distrust among the students as to who might work for SAVAK. They wouldn't know if any of their friends or acquaintances were SAVAK agents. They suspected each other terribly. This deep suspicion was reflected in a cartoon once in *Tufigh*, a satirical paper: a student is saying to a professor, 'Professor, although I agree with everything you say, I am afraid I still have to report you.' And the professor replies, 'If you do agree with me, why then do you have to report me?' And the student points to a fellow student saying, 'Because, if I don't report you, he will report me!'

People were watched and spied on at every level. Anyone who listened to any foreign broadcasts, mainly from the Soviet Union, or read any literature which was regarded as subversive, was suspect. Reading banned literature had to be highly planned. It would go like this. Three or four students would gather in a house, one would hang around near the front door, one would be in the middle of the house somewhere, and the third would sit in the farthest room in the house and read with the curtains closed. If anything suspicious occurred they would signal each other and the book would be hidden. If undesirable literature was found in the house it would carry heavy penalties.

In addition, rumours were rife about the royal family. For instance, about their sexual exploitation of others. It was said that whenever the Shah's brother, Ghulamreza, visited a girls' school, the prettiest girl would disappear from school the next day. It was said that the headmistress was approached on the spot for the girl's address, and that very night the girl was taken to the Court for Ghulamreza's pleasure. And that Ashraf, the Shah's twin sister, on military inspections, picked out the handsomest young men and ordered them to visit her for her sexual pleasure. The royal family was supposedly renowned for their sexual voraciousness and the supply of call girls from France was said to be unlimited.

When Ghulamreza Takhrie, a sportsman, a national hero, was murdered the story went round that he had been killed on the orders of the Shah's brother, whose name was also Ghulamreza and who was the sports minister. One day the Shah's brother had entered a sports stadium and no one took any notice of him, but when Ghulamreza Takhrie entered he was given a huge reception with such long applause that the Shah's brother was furious and ordered his murder. He was bundled up and taken to a hotel and given a lethal injection. A suicide note was left.

Dr Sadighi, my sociology teacher at the college, had been a close friend of Ghulamreza Takhrie. When he was asked what he thought of Takhrie's alleged suicide, he banged his fist on the table shouting 'Suicide! No man with his spirit would commit suicide. Who do they think they are kidding?'

Tufigh wrote at the time, 'Ghulamreza killed Ghulamreza!'

CHAPTER EIGHTEEN

The girls at the university hall of residence came from all over the country — students from Teheran itself lived at home — and they were middle class, with educated backgrounds, with the exception of one girl, Hamideh, and myself who both came from poor families. Hamideh's family had no formal education. She dressed simply — shabbily, as the other girls put it. She spoke quietly and asked many questions, funny ones at times, especially at the beginning. 'Why do they always serve lunch at half past twelve?' 'Well, what time do you suggest?' someone would take it up with her. 'Well, it could be twelve or one some days, couldn't it? Why half past twelve all the time, heh?' she would repeat, until someone would give her some sort of answer.

Her manners were simple and did not match those of the other girls. The story went round that at lunch the first day she drank soup out of a ladle rather than putting it in the bowl in front of her; this was regarded as a peasant mannerism. But the fact that she was suffering her own culture shock was not taken into account. She was a very bright, gentle girl, studying medicine.

At the Blind School, everything had been organized, arranged, laid down for us — every day the uniforms were ironed, the shoes were polished, we were transported to and from school, the food was cooked and so on, and we were never allowed out alone — but here, suddenly, I was thrown in the deep end, I was in Teheran, at the University, by myself and left to cope all on my own. There was only Hamideh with whom I felt anything in common.

People around me went out to the cinema, watched television, read comics, talked, laughed, enjoyed themselves, went to football matches, while I struggled with my day-to-day living. How was I going to pay for my expenses? How was I going to study without having help with reading? How was I going to deal with the exams? How was I going to get from A to B in Teheran? I felt unsafe, unsure, frightened.

Eventually, the Blind School sent me a typewriter and a tape-recorder. I found a part-time job, teaching English in a Blind School for two hours a day from two o'clock until four, every afternoon, except Fridays. I would travel to the school which was out of Teheran, an hour's journey each way. This school, called Reza Pahlavi, after the Shah's son, had only recently opened. Some of the teachers had been trained at my old school in Isfahan and it was through one of them, a good friend called Fati, that I got the job. The money I earned helped sustain me.

It was a residential school for both boys and girls aged from five to twenty. Older ones attended daily, mainly for workshops. It was the only blind school in the whole country run by the state. The man in charge of the school had absolute power. Anyone he didn't like suffered badly.

One of the students whom he disliked and had thrown out of the school, was a young man in his late teens with nowhere to go. He spent some nights out in the cold outside the gate. The winter was severe. One morning he was found dead in the street.

I enjoyed working with the children. I used to stay one night a week to look after them. Later, I spent some holidays there. In the college everyone was middle class. In the school, all the staff were middle class. I felt I was different from everyone else. Only with the pupils at the school did I have a point of identity. They were blind like me.

At the University, I taped the lectures, listened to them later and made notes in Braille. As for the books I had to read for my course, I arranged to read them with other students. They read the texts out aloud. As at school, I explained it back to them. We learned together, but they were able to revise afterwards for exams, and I was not, since it would have taken too long to take notes in Braille. Sometimes three or four of us studied together. At exams I sat in a separate room where I took down the questions in Braille and typed the answers. But this arrangement had its disadvantages. Sometimes teachers did not bother to arrange for me to take my exams at the same time as the other students, and would tell me they would deal with mine later. It would turn out that I had to sit three or four exams in one day. I did less well in exams than I should have, both because I was unable to revise properly and because of the way the exams were arranged.

My brother, Ali, tried hard to persuade me to go and live with his family and give the money I earned to him instead of using it for my lodgings. This I resisted. I knew he was only after the money. He and his family lived a long way from the University and it would have been impossible for me to travel to college and school on time. My brother told me I was uncooperative, thoughtless, wasting all that money on accommodation while he lived in such poverty.

People lived in extreme poverty and misery, especially in

south Teheran. My family weren't by any means the poorest. My brother with his wife, my mother (before her death) and my younger brother, all lived together in a house which consisted of one room ten feet square with cupboard-size storage space and a tiny yard of fourteen feet square, which had the toilet in one corner and a tiny pond in the middle. This house, with two other houses of a similar size, was in an alleyway two feet wide, down which just one person at a time could go. The land was bought from my uncle and they had built the house themselves. They were still paying for the land in instalments. The next-door house was occupied by an uncle of my mother's who had six children.

A river ran within a few yards of these houses which carried raw sewage and stunk terribly. When it rained heavily, the river flooded carrying away people's possessions, and sometimes causing death. People who lived along the river constantly lived in fear of their lives and for their children's health. Many diseases spread from the heavily polluted water. For years people had been campaigning to have the river cleaned or covered. Cleaning it was impossible they were told, it would be too expensive. Covering, the authorities would consider, and they had been considering it for years.

That year, 1966, the women had had enough. Something had to be done. They had seen their own children and children of their friends or relatives die from infections from the river. They had seen the bodies of many children carried away in its waters. One reason that women had so many children was that not many survived. The women formed themselves into a large group and, taking their babies and young children with them, marched to the town hall Shahadari, with a petition explaining what they wanted.

As they were not allowed inside they sat outside around the building. Traffic was brought to a standstill. Newspapers were alerted. The authorities had to take action. They agreed to cover the river. They could not call out the troops to open fire on a group of women and babies.

Many people lived in shelters made from whatever they could lay their hands on, bits of metal, plastic, wood, bricks, whatever they could find. This was especially so in south Teheran. There was a large quarry-like area called *Darvazeh Ghar* where people lived. Every so often bulldozers were sent to destroy people's homes and shelters. Once when homes were bulldozed, the women and children started crying and swearing at the people who had done it. 'Don't cry, don't swear at us,' shouted one of the drivers, 'but pray. Pray for an accident that prevents us from destroying your homes. We don't want to do this. We are under orders.'

I had friends who were teachers who told me disturbing stories about the children. One, Mehri, talked of a little girl in her class, a very bright girl who could not lift her head up from the desk one morning. 'What's the matter?' Mehri asked during the break, 'aren't you well?' 'I haven't eaten for days,' she replied, embarrassed. 'Look, I haven't eaten breakfast this morning either,' my friend said, 'I am rather hungry. I tell you what, I'll give you some money, go out and get some bread and yoghurt, and we'll have lunch together.'

'That's what we did,' she told me in sadness. 'They were all hungry. They didn't have any energy to study. They were all very bright, you should see them, eager to learn. My heart goes out to them.' In the winter they did not have enough clothing or shoes on their feet to come out in the snow. Those ones were the lucky ones — going to school.

CHAPTER NINETEEN

I had managed to secure a place in the hall of residence for the following year. By chance I met the Dean's secretary and she told me to go and see the Dean of the College officially in person. He understood my predicament. He spoke with the accommodation head, Mrs Mansoor, there and then. 'I don't understand why this girl was treated in this manner.' He was a kind man. I felt the concern and kindness in his voice as he spoke, as though he were ashamed that such a thing should happen. He arranged for me to stay at the hall of residence, and I had to sign a document, promising to pay back in instalments the University fees after I had completed my degree and started to work.

The Dean listened to me, sympathized, and gave me practical help; he even asked his secretary — a kind woman — to visit me every so often, to ring me, to keep an eye on me, which she did. One summer's day, she took me on a picnic with a friend of hers. She kept him informed of my welfare. This was very different from my experiences in the first year. This soothed, somewhat, my wounds.

The hall, a modern building, was on a fashionable street which ran at the side of the University and accommodated sixty girls. It was the only hall of residence for female students in Teheran. It had six floors. The rooms were mostly double, and on each floor there was one treble and one single room. The single rooms were initially built as kitchenettes, a communal place for girls to make tea and so on. Later, with the increased demand for accommodation, these rooms were converted to bedrooms, and as I was considered to have 'special needs', having to use a typewriter and a tape-recorder for my study, I was given one of these rooms. The other single rooms were given to foreign students, mainly students from Pakistan and some African countries.

The ground floor was used as communal sitting room, dining room and office. Three meals a day were served in the hall, with tea in the afternoon at four o'clock. There was a book kept downstairs and we had to write in it whenever we went out, saying where we were going and when we would be back. The evening meal was served at seven o'clock. If we had a legitimate college duty, such as work in the laboratory, dinner was kept for us; otherwise, if we were late, we did not get dinner. The warden, a Miss Bahaaddin, lived on the top floor. She was in her fifties, and was short, fat and always miserable. She grumbled and quarrelled with everyone all the time. 'And where do you think you're off to, Miss?' she would thunder suddenly. This was her good mood. She was filled with cynicism, sarcasm, suspicion. She was destructive, full of hatred, always. She walked heavily, and had a menacing aura about her. Girls referred to her as witch, giant, devil; everyone dreaded her terribly. She liked nobody, not even herself. Life seemed a hell to her and everyone had to suffer.

On Friday evenings the sheets were changed. We would take our sheets up to her floor and collect fresh ones. With me and Hamideh, she checked to make sure that our sheets were returned. She was suspicious that we might steal them. She terrified everyone as her heavy steps approached, her voice rumbling like thunder.

Mrs Mansoor came in daily to attend to the administration. We did not see much of her. She lived in the rich suburbs in north Teheran, and it was said that she had hired a young couple to come and do her housework every day. One morning she returned home unexpectedly to find the couple naked in her bed and she dismissed them both instantly.

I made sure that I ironed all my clothes before I put them on. Like other girls, I had to look good. People commented to my friends, 'This girl must have a maid to help her dress; not even her stocking seam is ever crooked.' One girlfriend said she was amazed at the things I did. 'I told my father,' she said laughingly, 'Monir picks up the tea cup from the exact spot where it was put down on the table.' Her father said, 'Probably she is deceiving you that she can't see.'

I was often either under-estimated or over-estimated. I found this infuriating, frustrating. Another friend, whenever she saw a needle in my hand, would take it from me quickly and do the sewing for me. 'I am frightened you might prick yourself,' she would say. 'I would rather do it for you than see you with the needle in your hand.'

Or a girl would say, 'I don't have to tell you what is out there, you can imagine, you've got a sixth sense,' as if I might have magical powers. 'You don't need *eyes*, do you?'

Veredeer, the friend who had travelled with me on the bus, was a kind, sweet, sensitive girl. During the first year we spent a lot of time together. We formed a deep friendship. We used to study together a lot. I used to go to her house or she came to visit me. One day she told me she had cancer. Within two years she had died.

Her death had a deep effect on me. I could not understand the tragedy, the cruelty. I witnessed the last moments of her life. She was in pain. Why did she have to go through that? Why did I have to lose her? She was a real friend, yet I had her for such a short time. I had depended on her, relied on her. We had confided in each other. She was able to talk to me more easily than to her four sisters. I felt privileged, lucky to have known her.

The girls who lived in the hall of residence had a difficult time with the authorities and their restrictions. What should they put in the book if they were going to take part in a sit-in, or political lecture in the evening? For the daytime they could put 'in the college', 'studying in the library' and such things. If they put they were going to a friend's or a relative's house, it would be checked.

Once, some of the girls disappeared for a few days. It was 1968. They had been detained and interrogated after student demonstrations, and we were surprised to see them return to the hall. Thereafter they were under pressure from their families, the hall of residence, University authorities, above all from SAVAK, to avoid any political activities.

Boyfriends were unacceptable. Those few of us who dared to make friends with boys had to be discreet, and at times deceitful: for instance a girl from Shiraz with whom I formed a friendship. One evening at a party in the hall for us newcomers, she noticed my anxiety and apprehension. She held my hand and took me up to her room and said, 'Do you feel like crying? Let's cry together!' I felt her cry in those words as she said them. A man visited her regularly; he was a good bit older than her. 'He's my uncle,' she told everyone. They used to sit for hours in the common room. The following year she married him.

This seemed like a good idea and I made an attempt to copy it. A male friend with whom I had corresponded for a long time, since schooldays, accompanied me back to the hall from an outing. We bumped into a group of people as we entered the hall. 'Hello! This is my uncle,' I said hurriedly. The next time I met my friend, he asked, 'How is your uncle?' 'But I meant *you* were my uncle,' I explained in astonishment. 'Ah! Thank goodness I didn't say anything then, because I thought you meant *he* was your uncle,' he said, referring to one of the men in the group.

I moved in several totally different environments: from the one in which my family were living — where eight people shared one room, and children were dying from malnutrition and cold; to the students' hall of residence where at night I was able to turn my radiator off with my toes to reduce the temperature of the room, feeling guilty knowing about those who could not keep themselves warm on severe winter nights. I also visited rich houses in Teheran where the people indulged in a lavish lifestyle, quite unaware of the sufferings of the poor. Those people lived in huge luxurious houses with swimming pools in their back gardens and expensive chauffeur-driven cars imported from abroad.

For instance, one family I met through missionary connections employed five members of a single family full time in addition to a chauffeur and a gardener. Such families employed nannies from the West. I met one nanny, an Englishwoman. She said her life in Teheran was like a dream, she had her own chauffeur-driven car and had just been given a fur coat for a Christmas present.

Not all the nannies were so lucky. I met another one, a black girl. Her lady hated her for her colour, degraded her and abused her often. She did not want her to swim in the same pool as her children. I never met such an unhappy person in that circle.

Discontent and frustration had been mounting up for some time in Iran among students, workers and intellectuals. Young people from the countryside poured into Teheran looking for work, just as my family had done a few years back. The country's agriculture was destroyed; previously Iran had been self-sufficient, now it relied upon food imports, mostly from the United States of America. It was widely thought that the United States' policy had been a deliberate one, intended to create dependency. Many peasants, forced to leave their villages, had moved to Teheran seeking ways in which to make a living. They worked during the day building hotels and villas for the rich, and at night slept huddled together in ditches or the abandoned quarries.

Boys as young as eight or nine years old worked long hours in the factories and sent the little that they earned to their families in the villages. One of them, a cousin, who was only ten when he started, worked in a tile-making factory and showed me the burn marks on his face. 'There is no protection from the fire,' he said. Girls worked as maids and prostitutes. I witnessed two sisters aged six and eight, who worked as maids, being spanked because they failed to keep the family's children, aged two and three, quiet while their mother attended to her reading of the Koran in the early morning.

Another relative told me that when he queued for a document outside a police station, it was midday and the sun was at its height. 'I was getting severe headache from the sun. I took a handkerchief out of my pocket and spread it on my head. It was a red handkerchief. A little later as I approached a door, the police officer sitting behind his desk in his air-conditioned office, noticed the handkerchief: "The one who's so careful about his head that he has put a handkerchief on it, get out of the queue now," he commanded. "It's only because the sun is giving me a splitting headache," I tried to explain, but it was no good, he insisted. I had to obey. I got out of the queue, took off the hankie, and joined the queue again at the end.'

People disappeared often. It was usual. There was a knock on the door in the middle of the night and they were taken away for questioning. People were detained, at times indefinitely, some were tortured: nails were pulled out; some had to lie down on metal beds which were heated gradually, and weights were hung from men's testicles. A friend's uncle to whom this was done later could not father a child. Rape, and inserting broken bottles into the rectum were common. A terrible joke went around among the young men: 'Do you want a Coke? Small or large?' 'Small, please. Less of a problem.'

Suspicion and fear ruled people's lives. We heard horrific stories about the kind of treatment people received in detention. Of girls who were reportedly raped and whipped. And of men, thrown into icy water in the night in their sleep, whipped naked, and of wild animals released into their cells. I heard of one man whose child was tortured in front of him, in order to get information from him about the activities of his friends, who kept saying, 'That child is innocent.' And many more.

Anyone could be picked up, any time, anywhere. Everyone knew this. People became deeply suspicious of one another. I had a friend with a cousin on the run. He rang at times, saying which direction he was taking to leave the country, in order to lay a false trail, knowing the telephone would be tapped. The friend's mother said, 'Go and give yourself up, Abas. How long do you want to live in this state, in hiding, homeless?' 'Give myself up! Do you know what they'll do to me if I did that?' He was caught in the end. He was executed. They had executed his father as well when he was a little boy.

One man I knew who had been in prison many times was losing his sight. They had shone extremely bright light into his eyes, it had damaged his eyes. People lived in terror and deprivation.

A relative who worked as a lorry driver took a load of bricks to Amirabad, the notorious prison. When he arrived at the entrance he was given strict instructions, 'Look straight ahead as you drive in and out, don't look to either side whatever happens. Do you understand?' he was told. As he drove in he heard the distressed cries of a man and glanced to the right, where the noise had come from. He saw a young man tied to a tree, naked, and being beaten savagely. The policemen with him in the lorry slapped his face, 'Didn't we tell you not to look?'

Someone else who worked with him once managed to speak to some of the young students in the prison, who handed him messages and the addresses of their families. On his way out he was searched and the papers were taken away. He was cautioned, and was very relieved not to be detained or punished. Military men of a certain rank had conscripts living in with their families; they were to help with equipment and clothing. These young men were doing their two years national service. Almost always they had to act as servants in the house. Many horrific stories of their treatment went round. I heard that one soldier who happened to turn his back on the master of the house as he got into the car was killed by an angry blow on the back of his head for not having the correct attitude.

Another soldier whose mother I knew starved to death. They were Turkish speaking immigrants from Russia, and the mother had worked as a nanny for years. Her son went to a house where he was treated appallingly. What horrified his family most of all, was the fact that he had to do all the washing, including the lady's underwear. Her knickers and bras he had to wash, one by one, by hand. Imagine that! In their view that was the worst thing that could happen to a man. And he was not given food for days on end; eventually he died, literally of starvation.

One day the Shah visited the University. He asked one of the students what he was studying. 'Economics,' the student replied. 'Economics?' the Shah repeated disapprovingly, 'What a useless subject. Why didn't you choose something useful? We don't need economists in this country.'

I remember one occasion when a factory in the north organized a march to Teheran; the workers were unhappy with their conditions. They carried in front of them a picture of the Shah, to show that they were not against him. As they marched towards Teheran the army was ordered to shoot; some workers died, many were injured and the rest turned back.

Students were always looking for ways to express their frustrations. Once they started smashing the windows of a cafeteria, yelling 'What kind of food is this you're giving us? We are not animals!' Another time after a sudden, steep rise in bus fares, demonstrations were organized. Students moved around in a large group shouting slogans: 'Freedom. Equality.' 'Justice for traitors.'

Quite often the police baton-charged the students on demonstrations. On one occasion I was with a friend from my class when the police started hitting out with their batons. The people next to us were hit but we were allowed to run away. 'It was because of you we were not hit,' my friend remarked. 'You see, it would make news if a blind student was beaten up.' But if students were seen with me, they could easily be identified because of my disability, so some kept their distance on demonstrations or at sit-ins.

Students conducted sit-ins in the University for long periods. Others would move around to stop or break up the classes. Some lecturers would ignore them and continue with their lecture and the students would shout, 'Come out!' 'Traitor, come out!' and persist until the lecturer left and the class broke up.

Dr Sadighi was a popular sociology lecturer, up to four hundred students would attend his lectures. Once when the class was in progress, the students arrived, opened the door and shouted, 'Justice' 'Equality' 'Freedom' 'We want action, enough of theories!' Dr Sadighi listened to them for a minute, then he came down from the stage and left the class. He got applauded for his response. He was sympathetic towards the students' cause.

He belonged to the National Front Party and had been imprisoned for a number of years by the Shah. When he was asked direct political questions he would remain silent. On one occasion though, he banged on the table with his fist shouting, 'I have been told not to talk!'

Student leaders were often rounded up and detained. Others would quickly take their place on demonstrations and carry on the protest.

I knew a group of students who had made a pledge to go to south Teheran regularly once a week to walk around among the poor to see the extent of poverty and the misery people lived in, so as not to forget, so as to keep their conviction for change strong.

The Shah's so-called White Revolution, white because it was meant to be bloodless, had had no real impact on people's lives. It was supposed to include land reform, a widespread literacy campaign, the enfranchisement of women, modernization of industry, redistribution of wealth, and a reduction in the power of the clergy.

In 1971 the Shah held a grand celebration to mark the anniversary of 2500 years of the Persian Empire (founded by Cyrus in the sixth century BC), his thirty years on the throne and the tenth anniversary of the White Revolution. This lavish celebration cost the country millions of pounds — according to one estimate, thirty million dollars — entertained statesmen and the richest from around the world and took place in Persepolis which is near Shiraz in the south of Iran. Food and tents for the celebration were supplied from France. In his speech at the celebration, the Shah said, 'Cyrus, sleep in peace, because Iran today is just as great as it was in your day!'

As I was travelling to Isfahan on a coach from Teheran, I heard two men sitting behind me discussing *Shahr Ghesseh*, a popular show with subtle but strong political insight, which reflected the continuing discontent and unhappiness of the people. I sensed that they themselves were involved in the show. I longed to talk to them about it. 'I know it.' 'I've heard it.' 'I loved it. I understand it.' I could not bring myself to talk to them. I was petrified that they might refuse me, reject me, ridicule me, and yet I felt they were such nice people. I was in such a dilemma. My feelings were confusing. Such strong feelings, wanting to communicate with them, the feeling that they were nice people, and yet the strong, counter-feeling that they would refuse me, ridicule me. I struggled with these feelings all the way, the whole journey, and for a long time to come.

When we reached the station, in Isfahan, they must have sensed my interest. They asked me where I wanted to go. I explained. They offered to take me in a taxi. No, I could not accept that. They insisted, gently. I could not trust them, they could not have accepted me as a person. I longed for their company, and yet I could not accept their offer. It left me burning inside with conflicting, strong feelings. I could not trust my own people. I could not take their trust, their acceptance when it was offered. This remained with me a very long time, I could not unravel it, understand it, make sense of it.

In 1970 I graduated from Teheran University with a BA in Psychology.

So Very English
Marsha Rowe (ed.)

Has Peanut Butter taken over from Marmite? Why do visitors flee from a barn owl called Maggie in Norfolk, or a rat called Oscar in Earls Court? Wasn't Zola really describing the English farmers rather than French peasants: all that land-grubbing and greed and rough lust in the ditches? Did Eliot sum it all up: 'The ferocious comedy of England with its peculiar mark of violence.' What about the typically English values of common sense and decency, helping and solidarity, rectitude, love of landscape? These and many other idiosyncracies of English life are looked at in this perceptive, witty short story compilation.

'A fascinating, funny and – if you are English – shaming anthology.'   *The Guardian*

Sex and the City
Marsha Rowe (ed.)

'Unerringly entertaining and thought provoking.'
JOANNA BRISCOE, *Girl About Town*

'The whole book opens into the category of good dirty fun, and is not the worse for that.'
ROBERT NYE, *The Guardian*

'A mixture of 1980s eroticism, sexual humiliation and an underlying wistful longing for the milk of human kindness, seemingly destroyed by urban living. Compulsive stuff.' *The List*

'Strangely intriguing.' *Glasgow Herald*

'There is no other collection quite like *Sex and the City*.' *TES*